UNITED THEY HATE

UNITED THEY HATE

WHITE SUPREMACIST GROUPS IN AMERICA

Michael Kronenwetter

Walker and Company

New York

First published in the United States of America in 1992 by Walker Publishing Company, Inc.

Published simultaneously in Canada by Thomas Allen & Son Canada, Limited, Markham, Ontario

Library of Congress Cataloging-in-Publication Data
Kronenwetter, Michael.
United they hate: white supremacist groups in America / Michael Kronenwetter.
p.   cm.
Includes bibliographical references and index.
Summary: Chronicles the development of white supremacy hate groups and analyzes their philosophies, personalities, motives, and weaknesses.
ISBN 0-8027-8162-4. —ISBN 0-8027-8163-2 (rein)
1. White supremacy movements—United States—History—Juvenile literature. 2. United States—Race relations—Juvenile literature.
[1. White supremacy movements. 2. Racism. 3. Race relations.]
I. Title.
E184.A1K84   1992
305.8'00973—dc20   91-39778
CIP
AC

Printed in the United States of America

2   4   6   8   10   9   7   5   3   1

Contents

1

The Heritage of Hate

Alan Berg was the host of a popular radio call-in show on station KOA, in Denver. KOA was a powerful station, and Berg could be heard in more than half the states in the entire country. He was famous for his combative style, which he used with callers and studio guests alike. Berg delighted in insulting people he considered ignorant, bigoted, or just wrongheaded: a large category that included just about everyone who disagreed with him about anything. He would often yell at guests, or hang up on callers in the middle of what they were saying.

Some listeners doubted that Alan Berg was really as hostile as he seemed. They thought that he sometimes said things he didn't really mean, that he faked a lot of his outrage to stir up controversy and build a bigger audience for his show. Maybe so. But one element of his outrage he didn't fake was the loathing he felt for white supremacists. Berg got many calls from these people, who claimed that the only real Americans were white, native-born Christians. Sometimes, he even had them on the show as guests.

The white supremacists argued that everyone who was foreign, or not white, or not Christian, was inferior. They insisted that all of America's problems were caused by immigrants, black people, Hispanics, Asian-Americans, Roman Catholics, and especially Jews. Some even expressed admiration for Adolf

Hitler, who had tried to murder all the Jews in Europe. Alan Berg had a very personal reason for being angry with people who hated Jews. He was a Jew himself.

Some of Berg's listeners loved him. Some hated him. Still others, he said himself, loved to hate him. But all of them tuned to listen to Berg do battle with his guests and callers. His show was the most popular talk show on KOA and one of the most popular local talk shows in the country—until the night of June 18, 1984.

That was the night Alan Berg died.

It was dark when he pulled his car up in front of his apartment around 9:30. He probably couldn't see the three men hiding in the shadows waiting for him, or the fourth man waiting in a parked car not far away. Opening his own car door, Berg paused to light a cigarette. One of the men stepped forward out of the darkness. He aimed a .45-caliber machine pistol point-blank at Alan Berg and pulled the trigger.

A .45-caliber machine pistol is a powerful weapon. The force of just one of its bullets would have been enough to knock Berg to the ground. But the gun was fully automatic. It fired so rapidly that ten bullets struck him before he hit the ground.[1]

The men who murdered Alan Berg were white supremacists. They belonged to a Nazilike organization that was sometimes called the Order and sometimes the Silent Brotherhood. As a result of outrages like the murder of Alan Berg, the Order would eventually be uncovered and destroyed. At least some of Berg's killers would be caught and jailed.

But the end of the Order would not mean the end of white supremacist hatred and terror. The Order was just one of many white supremacist groups dedicated to spreading the twin poisons of racism and violence. More than 200 such hate groups are active in the United States today.

WHAT IS A HATE GROUP?

A hate group is any organization whose policies or programs are based primarily on hostility toward one or more minority groups.

Any racial, religious, ethnic, social, or political minority can be the target for a hate group's bigotry. Typically, members of hate groups are not hostile to individuals because of what they do, or even because of what they stand for. They hate them because of what they *are*. Black. Hispanic. Jewish. Foreign. Homosexual. Whatever.

Like the Order, most hate groups believe in white supremacy: the idea that the "white race" is somehow superior to all other races and deserves to dominate them. The hostility their members feel toward other races and ethnic groups goes far beyond simple prejudice or even discrimination. A social club that refuses to admit people of certain races or religions discriminates against them, but it is not a hate group. Hate groups are not satisfied with merely discriminating against minorities. They don't just want to trample on their civil rights as Americans; they want to deny them their basic dignity as human beings. They want to humiliate them, if not destroy them altogether.

Some hate groups want to deport minorities or sterilize them to stop them from having children. Some call for physical violence against minorities, up to and including murder. The most extreme haters advocate actual genocide—the total annihilation of an entire racial, cultural, or ethnic group.

The haters give various reasons for their many hatreds. The Jews control all the money, they say. Black people are mentally inferior. Hispanic-Americans have too many children. Asians are sneaky. Immigrants of all kinds undermine American values. And so on. But the real reasons for their hatred are irrational. Even the haters themselves don't understand them.

ANCIENT PREJUDICES

One thing is clear. Today's hate groups did not invent bigotry. Racial, ethnic, and religious prejudice are at least as old as human history. Hate groups are only the products of these evils, not the cause. They are the rotten fruits of a long heritage of fear and hatred that began in prehistoric times and stretches all the way down to the present.

Cultural and ethnic prejudices have probably existed ever since people first began banding together into tribes. Archaeological evidence suggests that certain hunting tribes in ancient Europe looked down on those tribes that survived by fishing or by gathering roots, fruits, and berries. Some warlike tribes may even have carried out a kind of genocide against their more peaceful neighbors.[2]

Religious Bigotry

Even though all of the world's major religions preach love and brotherhood, time and again people have used religion to justify hating—and even killing—one another. In the Middle Ages, for example, the Christians who dominated Europe discriminated cruelly against the Jewish minority who lived there.

In some countries, religious Jews were persecuted for their beliefs. Those who refused to become Christians were sometimes burned at the stake. Even where Jews were not burned, they were often forced to live in neighborhoods specially set aside for them called ghettos. From time to time, there would be terrible pogroms, during which Christians would swarm into the ghettos, destroying or stealing Jewish property and beating, raping, and killing many of the Jews they found there. At various times, Jews were expelled from many European countries. When they were, their property was simply seized by the state.

During the same period in history, religion led to a whole series of wars, called the Crusades, between the Christian nations of Europe and the Muslim lands of the Middle East. These wars were fought with a special ferocity, because the soldiers on each side believed they were fighting for their God against the forces of the devil.

And the Middle Ages are not unique. The history of the world is filled with many other cases in which religion has been used as an excuse for hatred rather than love.

Racial and Cultural Bigotry

Evidence of racial prejudice—judging people by the color of their skins—also goes back to ancient times. But, in the Western world at least, racism didn't become a major problem until the fifteenth and sixteenth centuries. That was the dawn of the colonial age, when the European nations first began sending explorers—and armies—to establish colonies around the world. The people they found in those distant lands were very different from themselves, not only culturally but in the color of their skins.

Militarily and scientifically, the Europeans were much more advanced than the natives. (A "native" is anyone who was born in a particular place.) Because of this technical superiority, the Europeans tended to assume that they were superior in other ways as well. They took it for granted that they must be more intelligent than the natives, for example, and they assumed that this superiority was both natural and inevitable.

If they were so much better than the natives, they felt that they must be different from the natives in some very basic and important way. And they associated this invisible difference with the most obvious physical difference between them, the color of their skins—that is, with their race. In this way, cultural and racial prejudices often get mixed up together. It becomes difficult to tell the difference between them, if there is really a difference at all.

Europeans were not the only ones who were prejudiced, either racially or culturally. The natives were often as prejudiced against the pale newcomers as the Europeans were prejudiced against them. This was dramatically demonstrated in the sixteenth and seventeenth centuries, when shipwrecked European sailors first began to wash up on the shores of Japan.

In this case, neither the Europeans nor the Japanese were obviously culturally superior to the other. Both societies were quite advanced for their times. They were, however, very different from each other, and each was used to dealing only with other cultures that were relatively backward compared with their own. As a result, when they met, each tended to assume that it was superior to the other.

The Europeans arrived in Japan confident of their superiority over anyone they might find in the distant corners of the earth, and Japan was the most distant corner imaginable. The Japanese, meanwhile, had been totally isolated from Europe, and most of the rest of the world as well, for as long as they could remember. They thought of their island as the center of the world, and they were not very interested in exploring anywhere else or meeting people from other places.

The prejudice that each group felt toward the other was only partly racial. It was not so much their different skin colors and physical features that caused the greatest prejudice between them. It was their strangeness. The vast cultural gulf between them made it difficult for the Japanese and Europeans to sympathize with one another, to recognize one another as brothers and sisters.

The Japanese considered the Westerners uncultured, even dim-witted. The mental slowness of the newcomers was proven by the fact that they found the Japanese language almost impossible to learn. The Europeans had no manners (by Japanese standards). They failed to show a decent respect toward Japanese women or even toward the Japanese nobility. In some ways, the Europeans hardly seemed human at all. They tended to have a lot more hair on their bodies and faces than the Japanese, seeming more like animals than human beings. Worst of all, the barbaric Westerners were filthy. They did not even try to keep themselves clean. For some reason, they seemed to be almost afraid of taking baths, and so they were always dirty and foul smelling.

On the other hand, the Europeans thought of the Japanese as odd, exotic creatures. Physically small, they sometimes seemed to the Europeans to be little more than children. They governed their behavior by an elaborate system of rules and traditions that made no sense at all to the Westerners. They spoke an odd, silly-sounding language that seemed (to European ears) to be made up almost entirely of squeaks and grunts. They knew nothing of Western science or technology. Although they lived on an island, they knew little about building or sailing ships. And (the most peculiar thing of all) they were in the habit of taking frequent baths, a reckless and foolhardy practice the Europeans considered dangerously unhealthy.

Ultimately, as elsewhere in the world, the prejudice each group felt toward the other came to be seen as racial. The Japanese were the way they were because they were "yellow" skinned. The Europeans were the way they were because they were "white."

Racial prejudice came in handy for those European nations that had colonies. It helped them justify what amounted to a massive theft of natives' lands all around the world. After all, the Europeans told themselves, since they were naturally superior to the natives, they must have the natural right to rule over them. They brought this attitude with them when they came to colonize what is now the United States. We are still feeling its effects today.

HATE GROUPS TODAY

Alan Berg's death was one outgrowth of this long heritage of hate. It is a bitter heritage that continues to divide people, group from group, nation from nation, race from race. Now, as always, it appeals to the weakest elements of human nature: resentment, suspicion, and cruelty. And, most of all, it appeals to fear.

In the United States today, that long heritage is most violently represented by the white supremacy hate groups. All of the ancient prejudices are echoed in the beliefs of hate groups and their members. Like the tribespeople of ancient Europe, they fear and resent foreigners, and almost everyone else who is noticeably different from themselves. Like the European colonizers, they associate different cultures and skin colors with inferiority. And, like the persecutors of the Jews in the Middle Ages, some of the most vicious of them call themselves Christians and proclaim their hatred in the name of God.

Many of today's hate groups are very small. They have only a few members, most of whom live in the same community. Others are very large, with thousands of members all over the country. There are many other differences between them as well, both in their beliefs and in their actions. In the end, however, all the differences taken together are less important than the similarities, for at bottom, all these groups are the same. They are all part of the same movement: a crazy quilt of hate, which seeks to spread racial, religious, and ethnic turmoil throughout society.

It is vital that every American—and young Americans most of all—become aware of the white supremacy hate movement and recognize it for what it is. It is particularly important to understand the threat these groups represent to the ideals of tolerance and individual freedom fundamental to the American way of life.

2

"We Hold These Truths"

The United States was founded on a great ideal. That ideal was best expressed by Thomas Jefferson in the Declaration of Independence: "We hold these truths to be self-evident, that all men are created equal, that they are endowed by their Creator with certain unalienable Rights, that among these, are Life, Liberty, and the pursuit of Happiness."

These are not just the opening words of the nation's first founding document; they are the most fundamental. They set forth the great vision of human liberty and equality that this country has been striving to live up to ever since.

Jefferson was not the first person to declare that "all men are created equal." Great philosophers and religious leaders had said much the same thing many times before. But the United States was the first country that set out to turn that ideal into a reality.

Ironically, some of today's most vicious hate groups wrap themselves in the American flag. They claim to be patriots, who want to protect the "purity" of the American way of life by freeing it from "foreign" or "un-American" influences. By that, they mean the influence of all racial, ethnic, and religious minorities.

In reality, nothing could be *more* un-American, more truly foreign to the American way of life, than to try to free America of such "foreign" influences, since that is precisely what America is: a collection of foreign influences.

A NATION OF FOREIGNERS

From its very beginnings, the United States has been a land populated by foreigners. As John F. Kennedy pointed out in his book *A Nation of Immigrants,* written two years before he was elected president: "Every American who ever lived, with the exception of one group, was either an immigrant himself or a descendant of immigrants. The exception? Will Rogers, part Cherokee Indian, said that his ancestors were at the dock to meet the Mayflower."[1] Today most scientists believe that the ancestors of Native Americans were themselves immigrants, probably from Asia.

Despite the impression some people have, most of the early explorers and settlers of North America were *not* pale-skinned Protestants from England. The Spanish were the first to colonize most of the New World, including Florida and the American Southwest, as well as most of South America. It was Hispanic Roman Catholics, not British Protestants, who established the first Christian churches in North America, as well as the first theaters and schools, and even the first American university. The French were the first to explore most of the rest of what is now the United States, while the Dutch founded the colony of New Netherlands, the Swedes founded New Sweden, and so on.

The ethnic diversity of North America was already well established 300 years ago. Eighteen different ethnic groups were already living in New Netherlands by the time it was divided into the colonies of New York and New Jersey in 1664![2]

Religious as well as ethnic minorities played a large part in the settling of the American colonies. Several of the colonies, in fact, were founded by unpopular religious groups looking for a place to practice their religions however they wanted to. Many thousands of Catholics, Jews, Quakers, Mennonites, and others whose religions were persecuted elsewhere found their way to the American colonies.

Non-British minorities of all kinds played important roles in the American Revolution. Among the many other possible examples: a black man was the first victim of the Boston Massacre; there was a Polish Legion in the Revolutionary army; and a Portuguese Jew named Hyam Saloman was one of the Americans' bravest and most valuable spies.

THE "AMERICAN RACE"

From the start, the new country was intended to be a daring experiment. It would develop a new form of government, one that would serve as an inspiration to people around the world. And it would grow a new kind of population to live in it.

As early as 1782, a French-born observer named J. Hector St. John Crèvecoeur declared that "the race now called Americans" was producing "the most perfect society now existing in the world." But what was this new race called Americans? It was, of course, not a race at all. It was a mixture of people of different racial, and ethnic, and religious backgrounds. It was, as Crèvecoeur put it, a "strange mixture of blood which you find in no other country. . . . Here individuals of all nations are melted into a new race of men whose labors and posterity will one day cause great changes in the world."[3]

Even then, more than 200 years ago, Americans were finding their common identity in the very fact that their backgrounds were so different. Together, this "new race" of people "of all nations" built themselves a new society in the American wilderness.

No one racial or ethnic group established the United States. Mostly Scots-Irish pioneered the eastern mountains, Germans built the covered wagons that carried American pioneers of all nationalities to new homes around the continent, Swedes taught them all to build the log cabins they lived in when they got there. Mostly Chinese and Irish workers laid the tracks of the great intercontinental railroads that bound the country together in the nineteenth century. The labor of black slaves from Africa formed the basis for southern prosperity before the Civil War, and freed black men and women formed the base of the southern labor force in the century that followed. And all the while, wave after wave of immigrants from around the world were fueling American industry with their labor.

The new nation's culture was formed out of the cultures of

its many peoples. America owes its main language to England, but it is an English enriched with terms and phrases from a hundred other languages. America owes much of its music to Europe, and more to Africa. It owes much of its cooking to Italy, France, Japan, and China.

Many books have been written on the contributions particular minority groups have made to American culture: to American art, industry, science, education, and so on. But, in the most basic sense, it is pointless to single out the contributions of this group or that group. Every contribution ever made to American society has been made by a minority or by some combination of minorities, for that is what it means to be an American: to be the product of a culture that is a mixture of cultures—a "race" that is a "mixture of blood[s]."

BETRAYING THE VISION

Unfortunately, the United States has never lived up to its own great vision of tolerance and equality. Two groups, at least, were left out from the beginning. They were the Native Americans and African-American slaves. Both, as it happened, had darker skins than the Europeans and their descendants. Both groups contributed enormously to the culture and society that was being built but were denied most of the benefits that resulted from it.

Most of the pioneers who settled the North American continent considered the Native Americans "savages." They convinced themselves that the people they called Indians were not even fully human. They considered them only one step removed from wild animals and believed them to be lazy, vicious, and dishonest by nature. These beliefs made it easy for the settlers to take their lands away from them with a clear conscience.

Not all the white pioneers thought of the Native Americans this way. Some recognized them as fellow human beings and considered them morally equal to whites. Some respected, even admired, many aspects of Native American life. Among the admirers were some of the founding fathers, who based certain features of the U.S. government on the democratic practices of some American tribes. Still, even most whites who accepted the Native Americans as full human beings also accepted the "right" of the Europeans and their descendants to dominate the continent that had been their home.

In some places, the newcomers "bought" the lands from Native Americans. Typically, the whites, who thought of Native Americans as dishonest, paid them much less than the land was worth and often proceeded to cheat them out of even that. In other cases, the whites simply grabbed the land without any payment at all.

The U.S. government was a willing participant in this take-over of Native American land. Several American presidents, including Thomas Jefferson and Andrew Jackson, supported the policy of "removing" Native Americans from their home-lands. Tribes who resisted were crushed by force of arms. So many people in some tribes were killed that the tribes ceased to exist at all, in what amounted to genocide. Those who survived were confined to reservations, or driven farther and farther west, until they had no place left to go. In this way, the whites moved all the way across the continent, driving the Native Americans from the lands that had been theirs for centuries.

Like Native Americans, black slaves were denied their de-served place in the American vision. How could this be? How could this "new race" of Americans—who thought of them-selves as a good and moral people—deny to others the very rights and freedoms they had fought a revolution to win for themselves? The answer was racism.

Racial prejudice made it possible to think of Native Ameri-cans as less than human, and of African-Americans as property. Without racism, slavery could not have survived for long in America. The practice went hard against the grain of the American moral and political tradition. It meant denying peo-ple their liberty, and liberty (like equality) was one of the principles the new country was founded on.

If the blacks were not really people—or were people of an inferior kind—then slavery might be acceptable for them. It might even be *good* for them. Some supporters of slavery quoted the Greek philosopher Aristotle, who had argued that "those who are so much inferior to others as . . . beasts [are] to men, are by nature slaves. . . . [L]ike all inferiors," he had suggested, they would benefit "from living under the rule of a master."[4] Some even argued that slavery was justified as a way of converting the "heathen" Africans to Christianity.

In reality, of course, slavery was never meant as a favor to the slaves. Nor was slavery *caused* by racism. It was caused by economics. This is shown by the fact that slavery, which at first existed in all the American colonies, only lasted in the South, where the economic reasons for using slaves were strongest. But although racism didn't cause slavery, racism made slavery permissible.

Many of the founders who attended the Constitutional Convention in 1789 hated slavery. They wanted it outlawed in the Constitution itself, but most southern delegates wanted their "right" to own slaves protected in the same Constitution. They insisted that they needed slaves in order to operate their farms and plantations. The two sides made a compromise. Slavery would be allowed to continue, but the slave trade that imported new slaves into the country would be abolished within twenty years.

In the end, the Constitution neither forbade slavery nor protected it. The word "slave" did not even appear there. Abraham Lincoln believed that this was because the antislavery delegates to the Convention were so appalled by slavery that they didn't want any acknowledgment that it had ever existed in their new country to contaminate that document.[5]

Slavery continued to arouse controversy as long as it existed. Southerners kept insisting on their "right" to own slaves, while in the North the dislike for slavery kept growing stronger and stronger. By the 1850s, Daniel Webster, the golden-tongued statesman from New Hampshire, was declaring that slavery had "arrested the religious feeling of the country" and had "taken strong hold on the consciences of men."[6]

The question flared up every time a new state or territory was added to the Union. Would it be slave or free? The South insisted on having as many slave states as free ones. Southerners worried that if the free states ever became a majority, they would outlaw slavery throughout the Union. The opponents of slavery, on the other hand, bitterly opposed the expansion of slavery anywhere. For decades, an uneasy balance was kept. But, as Lincoln finally realized, the country could not remain forever half slave and half free.

As long as it did, however, the federal government consistently supported the rights of the roughly 400,000 white slaveowners and denied the rights of their roughly 4 million slaves. As far as the government of the United States was concerned, those 4 million men, women, and children—about one-third the entire population of the southern states—were not really people at all.[7] They were property.

THE FIRST AMERICAN HATE GROUP

Even before the Civil War freed the slaves, some Americans were trying to exclude even more groups from the American vision of equality and freedom. Their attack was directed against the life's blood of America's culture and economy—new immigrants.

Anti-immigrant feeling began to show itself in the 1840s. At that time, a flood of newcomers from Ireland, Germany, and Scandinavia was pouring into the rapidly growing country. Americans whose own ancestors had arrived only a generation before began to resent the new arrivals.

The Irish spoke English with a heavy foreign accent. Most of the Germans, Swedes, and Norwegians spoke no English at all. Their difficulty communicating made them seem ignorant or slow-witted to many Americans. Many of the immigrants worshiped in "foreign" (usually Roman Catholic) churches. And, since they came with little or no money, they were forced to live in the filthy slums of the big cities, where living conditions were miserable, disease was raging, and work was hard to find. This led to charges that the newcomers were not only unclean and unhealthy, but lazy to boot.

Arriving immigrants were often taken in hand by local political machines, who helped them out and then told them how to vote. This led members of opposing political groups to think of the immigrants as politically corrupt as well as culturally inferior.

But the underlying reason for the growing hostility to the immigrants was the fear that they would take jobs, land, and resources away from "real" Americans. Some of those who felt that way pushed for tough laws to restrict new immigration and to limit the rights of the "foreigners" already here. Others took more direct action. There were violent anti-immigrant riots in Philadelphia and other cities. Catholic churches were burned. Innocent immigrants were terrorized, beaten, and sometimes even killed by "nativist" mobs.

In 1845, nativists organized the Native American party. (Its name refers to native-born white citizens, not to the indigenous peoples of North America.) Sometime around 1850, nativists in the East formed what can be regarded as the first significant hate group in American history, a secret society called the Supreme Order of the Star-Spangled Banner. Its goal was to rid the United States of "foreign" ideas and influences. In the meantime, it wanted to keep all "foreigners" and Catholics from holding political office.

Nativism grew into a powerful political movement, but since groups like the Supreme Order were secret, members usually denied knowing anything about them. This earned the whole movement the nickname the Know-Nothings. In 1854, the Know-Nothings began calling themselves the American party. They elected governors in Massachusetts, Delaware, and four other states, as well as several congressmen. They also achieved a majority in some state legislatures.[8]

The Know-Nothings were divided and finally destroyed by the same issue that almost destroyed the entire country: slavery. Most southern Know-Nothings favored slavery, while most Know-Nothings in the East and West opposed it. When the American party dodged the issue, many of its antislavery members went over to a new antislavery party, the Republicans.

The Republicans welcomed the nativists but not the nativism. Abraham Lincoln, for one, was uncomfortable with the anti-immigrant prejudice. "As a nation," he complained, "we began by declaring that 'All men are created equal.' We now practically read it, 'All men are created equal except Negroes.' Soon, it will read, 'All men are created equal except Negroes, and foreigners, and Catholics.' When it comes to this, I shall

Nativism and violence went hand in hand from the beginning. This lithograph portrays an anti-Catholic riot in Philadelphia on June 7, 1844.
LIBRARY OF CONGRESS

prefer emigrating to some country where they make no pretense of loving liberty."[9]

The American party ran the ex-Democratic president Millard Fillmore in the presidential election of 1856. But he managed to carry only one state and came in a distant third behind the Democratic winner, James Buchanan, and the very first Republican candidate, John Fremont. Within a few years, the Know-Nothings were finished as a political force.

It's not likely that the Know-Nothings could have survived for long anyway. Their party was based almost entirely on prejudice against foreigners, and members could never really agree on who was foreign. This problem was inevitable in a nation made up entirely of immigrants and the descendants of immigrants. Because of this confusion, Know-Nothings in different parts of the country embraced different groups as Americans. In the West, for example, German immigrants were welcomed into the fold, so long as they weren't Catholics. In the South, on the other hand, Catholics were allowed to join, but not if they spoke with a foreign accent, German or otherwise.

The Civil War spelled the end of both the Know-Nothings and slavery. Within five years after the war, the Fourteenth and Fifteenth amendments granted the full rights of American citizenship to "all persons born or naturalized in the United States." The American ideal was finally being extended to include all Americans, whatever their race, religion, or ethnic background—or so it seemed.

In fact, America continued to fall short of its ideal. In practice, Native Americans, black Americans, and other non-white Americans were still not fully welcomed into American society. What's more, nativist prejudice did not die out, despite the collapse of the Know-Nothings. Near the end of the nineteenth century, laws were passed that restricted the immigration of specific racial and national groups into the United States. Even today, there are limits on the numbers and kinds of people that can come into the United States.

The United States has never fully kept the great promise enshrined in the Declaration of Independence, but that promise has been—and remains—central to the American spirit. To a great extent, it defines what "America" is.

The effort to make that promise a reality has been going on since the Declaration was written. It goes on today. In that great struggle, the hate groups have always been lined up on the other side. Historically, none has been as large, as destructive, as powerful—or as violent—as the Ku Klux Klan.

3

Hatred on Horseback: The Night Riders of the Ku Klux Klan

The Ku Klux Klan is a many-headed monster. Its name and image have been used by many different groups, some large and some small, some content to talk and bluster, others incredibly violent and vicious.

Founded in the South just after the Civil War, the Klan's history has been a roller coaster of growing power, rapid decline, and reemergence. During its heyday in the 1920s, the Klan claimed 5 million members.[1] At that time, Klan chapters—called klaverns—were scattered across the country, from upper New York state to California, as well as throughout the South. Today's membership is much smaller, but the KKK's infamous trademarks—the sheet, the hood, and the burning cross—remain powerful symbols of racist terrorism and white supremacy.

THE BIRTH OF THE KLAN

The many evils of the Ku Klux Klan sprang from an almost innocent beginning. The original Klan was founded by six young veterans of the Confederate army, on Christmas eve night, 1865, in Pulaski, Tennessee. They called their group the Kuklos Clan, after the Greek word *kuklos,* which means circle. Someone thought it would be clever to spell the name "Ku Klux Klan," making it almost a parody of the names of college fraternities, which are often formed out of three letters of the Greek alphabet.

They invented elaborate rituals for their club and pretentiously humorous titles for the officers. The leader was the Grand Cyclops, the secretary the Grand Scribe. Some of the titles had an eerie ring to them. Messengers were known as Nighthawks, for instance, and rank-and-file members as Ghouls. They decided early on that the group's membership and activities would be secret. It would be more exciting that way. Besides, secrecy would make it easier for the young men to do mischief, and mischief seems to have been mostly what they had in mind.[2]

Klansmen dressed up in outlandish costumes, throwing sheets or robes over themselves to hide their clothes and wearing comical masks and pointy hats to disguise their identities. Then they tore through the streets of Pulaski on horseback, enjoying the looks of astonishment they got. Astonishment, and fear.

Before long, they were amusing themselves by frightening black people who lived in the area. Like most southern whites, the Klansmen resented the ex-slaves freed by the war. They were a constant reminder of the South's humiliating defeat. They particularly resented those black people who acted as though they should now enjoy the same rights and freedoms that white people had always enjoyed. They may have been forced to free their slaves, many white southerners insisted, but they would never accept them as equals.

In the days of slavery, night riders on horseback had patrolled the backroads around the slave cabins, searching for escaping slaves. Some plantation slavemasters even employed people to dress up as ghosts and ride out to the shanties where the slaves were housed. They would make lots of noise, hoping to convince the slaves that there were ghosts about, ready to pounce on anyone foolish enough to venture out into the darkness.

The Klansmen took a leaf from the slavemaster's book. Dressed in robes, hoods, and wildly decorated masks, they rode out to the isolated homes of rural black families. Joseph Gill, a black man from Huntsville, Alabama, once described these visits to a congressional committee: "They had gowns on . . . that came down to their toes, and some would be red and some black, like a lady's dress . . . and you couldn't see none of the face nor nothing: you couldn't see a thing of them. Some of them had horns about as long as my finger, and made black. They said they came from Hell; that they died at Shiloh fight and Bull Run. . . . They said they wanted [my horse] for a charger to ride into hell. . . . They said they came from Hell and wanted to ride him back to hell."[3]

Some of the freed blacks may actually have had a superstitious fear of Confederate ghosts. Others had a very realistic fear of the living white men under the hoods and the sheets, for it soon became clear that any black person who defied the Klan risked being whipped, badly beaten, or worse.

Word of the Klan's activities spread, and new chapters began to spring up elsewhere in the South. More and more men joined to get in on what they probably thought of as the fun. Most of them were young, and many were veterans of the war. Some, like the original founders, were well educated and relatively well-to-do. Others, however, were not. All were attracted by the excitement of the Klan—by the romance of the exotic costumes, the exhilaration of the secret night rides, and the sense of power they got from terrorizing people weaker than themselves.

As the months went by and the Klan grew larger, the activities of some Klansmen grew increasingly violent. But the Klan remained little more than a collection of rowdy bullies. It might have stayed that way, had it not been for the drastic Radical Reconstruction laws passed by the U.S. Congress in 1867.

RADICAL RECONSTRUCTION

Many northern Republicans thought the South was getting off far too lightly after the Civil War. After all, the South had carried out a rebellion that had cost the country an uncounted fortune and hundreds of thousands of lives. These so-called Radical Republicans considered the ex-Confederates traitors and opposed accepting them back into the nation's political life.

Moreover, they believed that the country owed black people

A rare sight today, and one that freed slaves, scalawags, and carpetbaggers hoped never to see—a Klansman in full regalia. The costume dates from around 1870, although the photo itself was probably taken in 1882.
COURTESY OF THE NORTH CAROLINA DIVISION OF ARCHIVES AND HISTORY

a full place in American society. They suspected that without federal control the white southerners would find some way to return them to virtual slavery. That suspicion was proven right in 1865 and 1866, when the southern state legislatures began passing the Black Code laws. These laws set up a variety of legal devices that forced the freed blacks to work under conditions not much better than those they had suffered under as slaves.

The U.S. Congress answered the Black Codes with a variety of federal measures to protect blacks' rights. These included the Civil Rights Bill of 1866, which granted ex-slaves full U.S. citizenship and gave the federal government the power to interfere in state affairs to protect them. Having won overwhelming control of Congress in 1866, the Radical Republicans passed the sweeping Reconstruction Acts of 1867 over President Andrew Johnson's veto. These acts put much of the South under federal military command. Federal military commanders were ordered to see to it that all eligible male voters, black as well as white, were officially registered. Even then, the southern states would not be allowed to elect their own governments until they enacted new state constitutions guaranteeing the rights of black people.

This so-called Radical Reconstruction amounted to a military occupation of the southern United States. Many Republicans felt this was just what the South deserved. After all, it had staged a military uprising against the U.S. government. What did southerners expect? But most southern whites were outraged.

Radical Reconstruction meant that political power in the South passed to three categories of people, all of whom were unpopular with most white southerners. The first group was made up of southern whites who'd opposed breaking with the Union all along and who had now become Republicans. Most of their fellow whites, who called them scalawags, considered them traitors to the South. The second group were called carpetbaggers: they were white Republicans from the North who moved south after the war to seek their fortunes. The largest, most resented of the three was made up of freedmen, the male ex-slaves now able to assert their political rights for the first time.

Because freedmen were now allowed to vote, and many "un-Reconstructed" white southerners were not, many blacks were elected to office in the South. Mississippi had two black U.S. senators, and no less than twenty black men were elected to the Congress from southern states.[4] Many black local officials were also elected. In some places in the South, blacks were actually governing whites, a humiliating situation for white southerners raised to think of black people as little more than animals. Some of the most confused and angry whites turned to the Klan as a means of expressing their outrage.

Where before, the Klan's violence had been more or less random and undirected, now the KKK could claim to have a purpose: fighting Reconstruction and everything it stood for.

THE DEFENDER OF WHITE SUPREMACY

By the spring of 1867, the KKK was no longer just a local organization. Membership had not only swelled but had spread throughout the South. Even the name had expanded. The group now called itself the Invisible Empire of the Knights of the Ku Klux Klan.

The Invisible Empire held its first big convention in Nash-ville in the spring of 1867. The convention elected Nathan Bedford Forrest to the new post of Grand Wizard, which was now the Klan's highest office. (Other new offices included Grand Titan, Grand Giant, Genji, and Fury.) Forrest, who had been one of the most colorful Confederate generals during the war, gave the Klan a new prominence and respectability in the eyes of many southerners.

The convention was held in secret, but it issued a public declaration proclaiming its devotion to a range of noble purposes. After announcing its loyalty to the Constitution of the United States, it promised to "protect the weak, the innocent, and the defenseless," to "relieve the injured and oppressed," and "to succor the suffering."[5] But the weak, innocent, injured, oppressed, and suffering the Klan had in mind were all white. It barred from membership anyone not committed to *oppose* "social and political equality for Negroes."

The flamboyant Civil War general Nathan B. Forrest was elected Grand Wizard of the KKK in 1867 and ordered it disbanded in 1869. LIBRARY OF CONGRESS

The real purpose of the Klan was clear. Its "fundamental objective," as spelled out in the 1867 declaration, was the "maintenance of the supremacy of the White Race in this Republic."[6] White supremacy has been the Klan's basic doctrine ever since.

Underlying the idea of white supremacy was a fear of sexual relations between black men and white women. At this time, there was not the kind of intense fear of "race-mixing" that would arise later. White men in the South had been having sex with black women (usually in the form of rape) for generations, and many children were born as a result. But this wasn't seen as a "race-mixing" problem because most of the children were simply considered black. Many a plantation owner's "stable" of slaves contained several of his own children.

Although sex between white men and black women was never openly approved of by respectable white southerners, it was widely tolerated. Yet the very thought of white women having sex with black men terrified most whites of both sexes.

A RAMPAGE OF VIOLENCE

Klan membership skyrocketed in the late 1860s, and so did its level of violence. The Klan's strategy for "maintaining the White Race" can be summed up in one word—terror. Klansmen went on a rampage of whippings, beatings, torture, mutilation, and lynchings across the South. One of their favorite weapons was fire. Fire could be used to chase an enemy from his or her home, to destroy a school where black children learned to read or a church in which a white minister called for racial equality.

Fire had an even greater power than its power to destroy. It had the power to terrorize. Fire was a horrifyingly uncontrollable force, particularly in rural areas, where there was no fire brigade and the only source of water might be a single well and a small bucket. Even better, from the Klan's point of view, fire conjured up powerful visions of hellfire in the minds of the superstitious.

Not all the Klan's enemies were easily frightened. Many brave blacks and whites alike defied the Klan. Some soon came to regret it, when they awoke to find their barns on fire or their homes burning down around them. Others were whipped by hooded mobs or dragged into the woods and lynched.

The Klan killed many white carpetbaggers and scalawags, but most of its victims were black. Klansmen had little to fear from attacking, or even killing, freedmen. Even those white law enforcement officials who disliked the Klan were often reluctant to bring whites to trial for crimes against blacks. If they did, a white jury was unlikely to convict the defendants.

The violence grew worse as the 1868 elections approached. There was no question which party the Klan was backing. The Democrats were campaigning for "home rule" for the states of the old Confederacy. The Republicans, on the other hand, had nominated Ulysses S. Grant—the hated general who had led the Union troops to victory over the South—for president.

As always, the Klan concentrated its most brutal attacks on its weakest and most vulnerable enemies. Its roughly 550,000 members launched a campaign of terror to keep as many blacks as possible from voting. As the elections drew closer, the toll on the freedmen became enormous. According to evidence presented to Congress, in the weeks leading up to the election, some 2,000 black people were killed in Louisiana alone. In some places, Klan murders were averaging more than one a day.[7]

Despite the Klan's best efforts, Grant was elected. One result of this bloodiest election in American history was an increased government commitment to curb the lawless brutality of the KKK. Both the Reconstruction governments of the southern states and the U.S. Congress began taking steps to end the Klan's reign of terror in the South.

The most surprising blow to the Klan came from within. In January 1869, General Forrest issued an order to disband the Klan. It was not clear why. Forrest himself may have become frightened that the Klan violence was getting out of hand; or he may have just been responding to the growing pressure from the state and federal governments. Or, as some historians suspect, the order may have been a smokescreen, which he never expected to be obeyed.

Whatever Forrest's motive, his order did little to end the violence. While it succeeded in dismantling the overall structure of the Klan, it failed to stop the terrorism. Local klaverns continued to operate. Klan night riders continued to roam the backwoods of the rural South, spreading terror and death in their wake. Fires continued to light up the night. Bodies continued to dangle at the ends of ropes by the side of country roads. If anything, Klan violence increased. There was no longer any overall formal organization to control it.

The Klan was not alone. Several other secret terrorist societies operated in the South. At least one, the Knights of the White Camellia, may have been even larger than the Klan at one time. There were also many less organized vigilante groups in towns around the South. These local groups, which had names like the White Leagues and the Red Shirts, sometimes managed to intimidate whole communities. Heavily armed, they bullied their fellow whites into voting Democratic and used terror to keep blacks from voting at all.

In 1871, President Grant ordered the Klan and all similar organizations to disband immediately. Congress enacted the Force Bills, which gave the government the power to use the military, if necessary, to protect blacks from violence. Assault, murder, and the other crimes most often associated with the Klan were made federal crimes. Congress even passed a special law directed specifically against the Klan itself. The wearing of masks, including hoods, was outlawed. Many Klansmen were arrested under these laws, but few were severely punished.

Oddly, opposition from the government wasn't what finally ended the Klan's reign of terror. It was success.

THE END OF THE KLAN

The presidential election of 1876 ended in a deadlock between the Republican candidate, Rutherford B. Hayes, and the Democrat, Samuel J. Tilden. The choice of a president was turned over to the U.S. House of Representatives. There, Democrats and Republicans made a compromise that would have a fatal effect on the hopes and dreams of black Americans in the South—and on the Ku Klux Klan. The Democrats agreed to let the Republican, Hayes, be President. In return, the Republicans agreed to end Radical Reconstruction in the South.

The result was that all serious federal efforts to protect the rights of black people in the South came to a sudden halt. Now in white control, the legislatures of the southern states quickly passed what became known as Jim Crow laws. These state measures imposed an elaborate system of legally enforced segregation (or separation) of blacks from whites. For nearly a century, Jim Crow would squash all hope for "social and political equality for Negroes" in the South.

Reconstruction was dead. Robbed of its greatest enemy, the Klan could only fade away. From the point of view of the white racists, there was no need for it anymore. Jim Crow would ensure the "maintenance of the White Race" in the South for a long time to come.

4

*Hatred for Fun and Profit:
The Most Successful Hate
Group in American History*

Although it seemed to die out at the end of Reconstruction, the Ku Klux Klan would prove to be the most persistent of all American hate groups. Like the restless spirits the early night riders had claimed to be, the Klan was destined to rise from its grave again and again. But the Klan was no unhappy Confederate ghost. It was more like a Jason, or a Freddie Krueger—an evil spirit, delighting in terror and death.

THE ENTREPRENEUR OF HATE

The first revival of the Klan took place in 1915. Two events occurred that year which would lead to the Klan's rebirth. The first was the enormous success of *The Birth of a Nation*, a remarkable movie directed by D. W. Griffith. Critics still consider it one of the best movies of all time, but it was shamefully racist.

Based on a novel entitled *The Clansman*, *The Birth of a Nation* presented the Reconstruction Klan as a band of noble heroes who saved the South from the hands of the carpetbaggers and scalawags, and pure white southern womanhood from the hands of brutish, black freedmen. There is no question of the movie's power. The film's racist propaganda was so effective that a scene in which a white mob lynched a black man drew rousing cheers from white audiences around the South.

Knowing little about the reality of the post-Civil War South, many people around the country accepted the movie's heroic version of the Klan as historically accurate. The good feelings the movie aroused toward the Klan turned out to be a lucky break for an ambitious young businessman named William J. Simmons, who had decided to launch a revived version of the Klan that same year. Simmons would prove, for the first time in American history, that hatred and racism could be turned into a profitable business enterprise.

Simmons was a heavy-drinking ex-preacher who had turned to selling insurance when he lost his pulpit for misbehavior. Casting about for some way to give meaning to his life—and to put some extra money in his pocket—he hit upon the idea of reviving the Klan. At first he conceived of it as a kind of combination spiritual society and drinking club. (Bars and taverns were outlawed in Simmons's state of Georgia, but men were allowed to drink alcohol at private clubs.) It would be, he boasted, "altogether . . . weird, mystical, and of a high class."[1] Eventually, he seems to have dropped the drinking-club idea and concentrated on the weird and the mystical elements of his plan.

On the night before Thanksgiving Day, 1915, Simmons and his first fifteen recruits rode a bus to the top of Stone Mountain, near Atlanta, Georgia. Standing on the summit, they set fire to a cross. It was the first official ceremony of the new, twentieth-century version of the Invisible Empire of the Ku Klux Klan.

From the outside, the new Klan looked a lot like the old Klan. Its members wore similar robes and hoods, conducted similar ceremonies, and called one another by the same strange titles. And, like the Reconstruction Klan, the new group was openly racist. A Klan publication frankly described the organization as "a White Man's organization . . . teaching the doctrine of White Supremacy."[2]

The similarities with the original Klan were a little misleading, however. Simmons's Klan was very different from the old Klan in many ways. It was less mean-spirited, for one thing—at least at first. Even its racism was hardly extreme by the standards of its time and place. (*All* fraternal brotherhoods in Georgia were segregated in those days.) Simmons's charter

The entrepreneur of hate, William J. Simmons, looking every bit the prosperous businessman he was. LIBRARY OF CONGRESS

from the State of Georgia officially licensed his group as a benevolent, or charitable, society. And, in fact, the new Invisible Empire had as much in common with such benevolent societies as the Oddfellows and the Lions Clubs as it did with the Reconstruction Klan.

If Simmons was going to attract a large membership, he had to give them a reason to join his organization instead of the others. The old Klan had attracted members by rallying them against a common enemy: Reconstruction. But Reconstruction was long dead. The South was now firmly in the control of southern whites, and blacks were kept firmly under whites' thumbs by Jim Crow.

Lacking an enemy to rally members against, Simmons put his emphasis on the positive values he shared with most white southerners, values he summed up in the terms "Americanism"

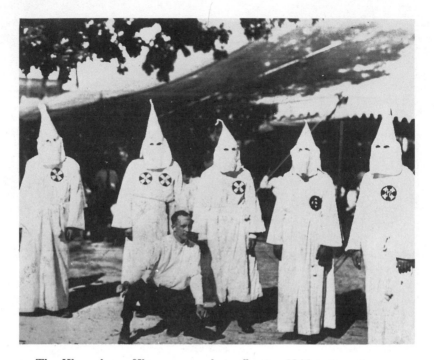

The Klan reborn. Klansmen posed proudly at a 1915 tent meeting near Hamlet, North Carolina. The robes and hoods were undoubtedly brand new, sold to them (along with an insurance policy) by Simmons or one of his kleagles. COURTESY OF NORTH CAROLINA DIVISION OF ARCHIVES AND HISTORY

and "Christian Civilization." In the eyes of most white southerners, the two terms described the same thing—the white society that existed in the rural South at that time. The values they embodied included white supremacy, private enterprise, and the kind of Protestantism preached in the fundamentalist churches of the area.

A belief in the supremacy of "the White Race" was only one of the dark sides of the new Klan's beliefs. The Klan also embraced a new version of nativism, and the religious bigotry that had always gone with it. For the Klan, as for the Know-Nothings, favoring "Americanism" meant opposing anything "foreign" or "alien." Favoring "Christian Civilization" meant opposing any religion that was not Christian—or, more specifically, not fundamentalist Christian. This included not only Judaism (which did not believe that Christ was God) but also Roman Catholicism. As the Klan saw it, the world's largest Christian faith was an alien religion, ruled by a foreign, Italian Pope.

The Klan's hostility toward everything foreign got even stronger after the United States entered World War I in 1917. The war also led the Klan to oppose organized labor, which it accused of hurting the war effort by taking part in strikes. The Klan and organized labor were natural enemies for other reasons as well. Many union organizers were immigrants, and some unions flirted with socialism, which the Klan regarded as a "foreign" idea.

Klan membership grew during the First World War but not enough to satisfy Simmons. He was making money from every new member who joined the Klan. He not only collected a ten-dollar fee from each of them but sold them a robe and hood and a life insurance policy to boot.[3] Simmons decided that Klan membership might be more attractive if it were secret, so he forbid members to admit their membership to anyone outside the Klan itself. Like the Know-Nothings and the old Klan itself, the new KKK had become a secret organization. The device worked. Klan membership began to grow faster.[4]

By 1920, Simmons's KKK had about 5,000 members. At ten dollars a head, plus profits on robes and insurance policies, Simmons's venture was paying off nicely. Yet the original Klan had once had more than ten times that many members. Simmons realized that he needed help if he wanted to turn his organization into a really big money-maker. He hired an Atlanta public relations firm, run by Edward Clarke and Elizabeth Tyler, to help build up his membership. They were the ones who recognized the full power of racism and ethnic hatred to attract new members. Guided by Clarke and Tyler, the Klan began to strengthen its claim to represent white, Christian America by emphasizing its hostility toward everything else.

The old Klan had claimed to be the protector of the southern way of life. Now, the new Klan began selling itself as the protector of the *American* way of life. As Simmons described it in a letter to potential members, that meant: "The Tenets of the Christian Religion, White Supremacy, Protection of Our Pure American Womanhood, Preventing unwarranted strikes by Foreign Labor Agitators, Upholding the Constitution of the United States of America, The Sovereignty of our States Rights," and "Promotion of Pure Americanism," among other things.[5] The Klan, Simmons now proclaimed, would work to "maintain Anglo-Saxon civilization on the American continent from submergence due to the encroachment and invasion of alien people of whatever clime or color."[6]

The Klan's philosophy had always had strong elements of bigotry in it. But now, as promoted by Clarke and Tyler, it became a full-fledged hate group, attacking everything it considered foreign, alien, or even different. Its enemies included not only blacks, Catholics, and Jews, but all so-called hyphenated Americans, such as Italian-Americans, Asian-Americans, Irish-Americans, and Swedish-Americans, as well as anyone else not firmly rooted in generations of "Anglo-Saxon civilization."

The Klan's new approach hit a responsive chord in rural and small-town America. The country had just been through World War I: a "foreign" war, which had killed thousands of young Americans for a cause many of them never understood. Farm crises in 1907 and 1914 had cost many small farmers their farms. Many of the farmers who were left lived in constant fear that the bank would call in the mortgages on their farms.

Immigrants had been pouring into the country for decades. Now they were coming at a rate of nearly half a million a year. Most were settling in the big cities. In 1920, for the first time in American history, there were more people in the cities than in the rural areas. This was an alarming reality for rural Americans, who had always thought of themselves as the heart and backbone of the nation. They had built this country. Their values—Christianity, hard work, and patriotism—had made it strong. Now, they feared, the country was slipping away from them. They failed to see that many of the immigrants, and Jews and black Americans as well, had similar values to their own.

A real sense of fear lurked beneath the peaceful-looking surface of rural America. There was an anxious feeling that alien forces were at work in the country. The Klan used this fear to propel itself into a position of power and influence in the United States. Led by Clarke and Tyler, it launched a major campaign for new members, based frankly and openly on bitter hostility toward all "alien" races and religions.

As a public relations move, this campaign was a stroke of genius. For rural and small-town Americans who wanted someone to blame for what was going wrong in the country, the Klan had the answer. All of America's troubles, the Klan explained, were caused by foreigners and other races, who were corrupting America with their alien ideas and corrupting the white, Anglo-Saxon race with their alien blood. The biggest villains of all, in Simmons's words, were the "Niggers, Catholics, and Jews."

Klan membership soared, skyrocketing from around 5,000 in early 1920 to nearly 100,000 by October and to more than 1 million the very next year. Unlike the old Klan, the new Klan wasn't exclusively male. A woman could pay the same membership fee as a man, and money was what the new Klan leadership was most interested in. Membership wasn't limited to the South either. Klan organizers called kleagles—traveling salesmen of hate—fanned out all over the country. Their nativist, anti-immigrant message found tens of thousands of sympathetic ears in the North, Midwest, and West. They appealed to local prejudices, emphasizing the Klan's stand against whatever the local white citizens feared and hated most, which included immigrants, blacks, Jews, and labor unions.[7] Ironically, the Klan, which Simmons had originally thought of as a drinking club, was even sold as a strong opponent of alcohol. Thanks to the hard-selling kleagles, the flaming cross became a familiar sight all the way from upper New York State to San Jacinto, California.

PAYING THE PRICE

The price of the Klan's success was paid by thousands of American blacks, Catholics, Jews, and new immigrants—and by many white Protestants as well. Local klaverns operated more or less independently, and their victims varied from one klavern to another. In addition to the groups the entire Klan considered un-American, local klaverns often set out to "punish" people they considered immoral as well. The list of the Klan's victims included many unfaithful wives, bootleggers, dope pushers, ministers who preached against the Klan—and in some places even white businesspeople who dared to keep their stores open on Sundays.

The punishment for being an enemy of the Klan varied widely. Some victims might have crosses burned on their front lawns. Others might be whipped, or tarred and feathered, or have the letters "KKK" branded onto their skins with acid. Still others were lynched.

The growing violence attracted widespread public attention. The New York *World* published a shocking series of articles exposing the Klan's terrorizing activities. A Georgia newspaperman named Julian Harris won a Pulitzer Prize for his daring editorials attacking the Klan, which he described as "a cowardly masked gang."[8]

In 1921, a congressional committee held hearings to investigate the Klan. Simmons was called as a witness. He denied that the national organization knew anything about the violence. Nothing much came of the committee investigation, except a lot of free publicity for the Klan. "The result was that Congress gave us the best advertising we ever got," Simmons later explained. "Congress made us."[9]

For Simmons, Clarke, and Tyler, the profits were enormous. By 1922, the Klan was collecting $10 million in membership fees alone. Millions more were pouring in from the sale of hoods, robes, and other Klan paraphernalia. In addition, the Klan was branching out into the publication of hate literature, and even into real estate. Simmons's business venture was finally paying off in a big way.

POLITICAL POWER

In some places, the Klan was little more than a nuisance. In others, it was powerful enough to control the whole community. A klavern whose membership included influential business and political leaders, along with enough roughnecks to do the leaders' dirty work, could become a kind of shadow government. In such places, the Klan really *was* an Invisible Empire.

For Simmons and the other national leaders, the Klan's financial empire was even more important than the political one. In the early 1920s, a kind of civil war broke out inside the Klan as high officials fought for control of the money. One by one, the original leaders disappeared. Elizabeth Tyler resigned for personal reasons. Edward Clarke, who had made his career promoting the Klan's Puritanical version of morality, was sent to jail on a morals charge. Finally, Simmons himself lost control of the organization to a Texas dentist named Hiram Wesley Evans. Yet through it all, the Klan kept growing. By 1925, the Klan was claiming 5 million members, millions of whom were in the North. The growing numbers meant growing political power. The Klan was establishing itself as a real force in national politics.

The Klan had little real political ideology. It went where the power was. In the North, the Klan usually allied itself with Republicans. In the South, which was solidly Democratic, the Klan worked through Democrats. Since Klan membership was secret, it's impossible to know how many public officials actually belonged to the Klan. Certainly hundreds of sheriffs, judges, and other local officials were members. It is likely that at least three state governors belonged. So did many congressmen (there were no congresswomen in those days) and at least one U.S. senator—Earl Mayfield of Texas. In any case, the Klan's political influence went far beyond its own members. Even many politicians who did not actually belong to the Klan willingly cooperated with it and did its bidding.

Outside the South, Klan power was particularly strong in Texas, Colorado, Arkansas, Oklahoma, Oregon, and Maine. For a time, the Klan's Grand Dragon in Indiana, David C. Stephenson, was the virtual political dictator of the state.

Klan influence was a major issue at the Democratic party's national convention in New York City in 1924. Northern Democrats, many of whom were Catholics or recent immigrants, wanted the party platform to condemn the Klan. Southern delegates, many of whom were Klan members themselves, were determined to keep New York's governor, Al Smith, who was a Catholic, from being nominated for president. In a bitter convention fight, the Klan won both battles. Al Smith lost the nomination, and the Democratic platform said nothing against the Klan.

The Democrats lost the presidential election to the Republican president, Calvin Coolidge. Having exercised a kind of veto over the Democrats' choice of a presidential nominee, however, Evans now claimed that the Klan had helped reelect Coolidge. The following summer, he called Klan members to Washington, D.C., to celebrate their power. Forty thousand of them came to march down Pennsylvania Avenue in the flowing white robes of the Ku Klux Klan. No one knew it then, but that would be the high point of the Klan's glory. The Invisible Empire was about to collapse.

THE DOWNFALL OF THE KLAN

The Klan's downfall was even more rapid than its rise and was brought about by the personal disgrace of one man: David C. Stephenson, the Grand Dragon and political dictator of Indiana. In 1925, he was tried and convicted of the murder of a young white woman. The case involved sordid sexual activities as well as violence and created a national scandal. The Grand Dragon was sentenced to twenty years in jail.

Stephenson had been the most important official in the Klan except for Hiram Wesley Evans himself. He and Evans had been rivals for power, and he was convinced that Evans's supporters had brought about his trial. Whether for revenge or to win better treatment from the authorities, Stephenson went public with the truth about the Klan's activities.

Stephenson admitted some of the Klan's worst acts of violence. In addition, he revealed the Klan's deep involvement in virtually every level of government in Indiana. Among other things, his revelations led to the indictment of both the governor of Indiana and the mayor of Indianapolis, who had served as tools of the Klan.

Most damaging of all, Stephenson exposed the true extent of cynicism, greed, and corruption that existed at the highest levels of the Klan organization. He revealed that the rulers of the Invisible Empire were more interested in profits than they were in any ideal of Americanism or Christian civilization. Investigations prompted by Stephenson's testimony soon uncovered a wide range of financial misdeeds by Klan officials.

It was the Klan's finest hour as 40,000 Klan members gathered in Washington, D.C., in 1925. Before the year was over, however, D. C. Stephenson was in jail, and by the end of the following year, Klan membership had dropped from 5 million to 2 million. LIBRARY OF CON-GRESS

In light of Stephenson's revelations, even the most loyal Klan supporters had a hard time believing the Klan was a noble organization. The knowledge that money donated to the cause by ordinary members (many of whom were poor) had been misused by the high-living Klan officials shocked rank-and-file Klan members. Many refused to pay their dues. Since the Klan was essentially a business, this was the most devastating blow of all.

In the meantime, public outrage was building against the Klan. People willing to overlook Klan violence, as long as it was directed against Catholics, blacks, Jews, foreigners, and union workers, were alarmed by the Klan's growing list of victims. Several states passed new laws outlawing Klan activity.

After reaching a peak of about 5 million in 1925, Klan membership plunged to a little more than 2 million by the end of 1926. By the end of 1927, it was down to a mere 321,000. And, because of its dwindling membership, the Klan was rapidly losing its political power. By 1930, membership had dropped to around 35,000.

During the Depression of the 1930s, what remained of the Klan focused most of its hostility on organized labor, communism, and the liberal New Deal reforms of the Democratic president, Franklin D. Roosevelt. According to Klan propaganda, Roosevelt was a Jew (he wasn't) allied with an international conspiracy of Jewish bankers, communists, and union leaders in a plot to destroy American business. All of this made little sense to many of the poor and uneducated people who had once been the Klan's main recruits. Most of them were glad of the New Deal's efforts to cushion the effects of the Depression. By the end of the 1930s, Klan membership had dropped to a pitiful 10,000 or so, almost all of whom were in Florida and most of whom were behind in their dues. The Klan's days as a big money-maker were over.

In 1939, a man named James A. Colescott took over the Klan from Hiram Evans. He did what he could to return the Klan to power and profitability, but what he did wasn't nearly enough. In 1944, the U.S. government sued the Klan for $685,000 in back taxes it said were due on profits the Klan had made almost twenty years before. Colescott was forced to turn over what was left of the Klan's financial assets. "Maybe the government can make something out of the Klan," he brooded. "I never could."[10]

5

The Klan's Losing Battle to Save Jim Crow

The Klan all but disappeared for a second time after its bankruptcy in the 1930s. During the 1940s, most Americans were distracted from their racial conflicts by the much greater international conflict of World War II. It wasn't until the war was over—and black Americans began demanding the rights that had been promised them at the end of the Civil War a century before—that the Klan reappeared. It was this second rebirth of the Klan that formed the basis for the Klan that exists today.

CRACKS IN THE WALL

The U.S. military had been segregated throughout the war. Nonetheless, the war gave black Americans the chance to show their value to the country, and they took it. On the battlefronts, they proved that they could fight as well as whites. On the home front, some 2 million of them went to work in the defense industry.

Having suffered and died as bravely as any other Americans, they now felt entitled to all the rights and privileges granted to white Americans. Inspired by their wartime experiences, black activists launched new efforts to win their rights after the war. It wasn't long before their efforts bore fruit. In 1948, President Harry Truman ended the official segregation of the armed

forces. Outside the military, however, the wall of legal separation of the races remained as high as ever.

The National Association for the Advancement of Colored
People (NAACP) attacked the wall in the courts. Segregation
had been accepted as legal since 1896, when the Supreme
Court ruled that having separate facilities for the two races was
constitutional, so long as the ones set aside for blacks were
"equal" to those reserved for whites. In practice, however,
facilities were never "equal." The ones for blacks were almost
always inferior.

Faced with the challenges presented by the NAACP, the
Supreme Court began to reconsider its position. In 1954, in a
landmark case known as *Brown* v. *Board of Education of
Topeka*, the Court reversed itself and ruled that racial segregation in the public schools was unconstitutional. "In the field of
public education," the Court declared, "the doctrine of 'separate but equal' has no place. Separate educational facilities are
inherently unequal."[1]

The decision struck terror in the hearts of white supremacists. If segregated schools were unconstitutional, what about
segregated restaurants, hotels, and theaters? Would the Court
demand that all these be desegregated too? If so, where would
it end? What about racial discrimination in employment? What
about the laws that kept blacks from moving into white neighborhoods? For the first time since 1896, the whole Jim Crow
system was in danger.

The idea of integration terrified some whites who were not
white supremacists. The thought of change was particularly
frightening in the South, where Jim Crow was a way of life.
Segregation ensured white economic and political dominance.
On every level of society, whites had always gotten the best
jobs, the best housing, the best public facilities. They even got
the best seats in buses and movie theaters. Wealthy whites
cherished segregation because it protected their privilege. Poor
whites clung to it because it gave them the only social standing
they had. No matter how downtrodden, ignorant, or otherwise
disadvantaged they might be, they were at least socially superior to blacks.

Many whites were determined to resist the new threat to
their special position in society. They considered the Supreme

Court's decision an attack from the North on their way of life, and they refused to accept it. James Eastland, a white U.S. senator from Mississippi, spoke for millions when he declared that "the South will not abide by or obey this legislative decision by a political court."[2]

In many places around the country—and virtually everywhere throughout the South—schools simply refused to integrate. The Court's decision had to be reargued and reenforced again and again, state by state, sometimes school district by school district.

White mobs greeted black children who tried to attend previously all-white schools. They shouted vulgar insults at the youngsters, threatened them, and even threw rocks at them. Ordinary citizens weren't the only ones who resisted. They were encouraged by important political leaders like Eastland and by thousands of state and local officials.

In Alabama, for instance, Governor George Wallace became a hero to segregationists by standing in the door of a white schoolhouse and refusing to admit black students escorted by federal law enforcement officials. He called out the state troopers to prevent black students from entering a high school in Tuskegee.

Even at the university level, progress was agonizingly slow. Riots broke out when James Meredith became the first black student to register at the University of Mississippi in 1962. Three people were shot to death in the mayhem, and fifty others were wounded. Federal troops had to occupy the campus just to stop the violence.

In the meantime, black activists, and some whites sympathetic to their cause, were pressing to end other forms of segregation as well. In 1957, Congress passed the first Civil Rights Bill since Reconstruction. All through the early 1960s, the courts kept striking down one Jim Crow law after another.

For die-hard segregationists, the handwriting was on the wall. In fact, the whole wall was coming down. Jim Crow was dying, but he would die a long and painful death. And, all the while, a resurrected Ku Klux Klan would struggle desperately to keep him alive.

THE RESURRECTION OF THE KLAN

Shortly before the *Brown* decision came down, a Georgia auto worker named James Eldon had tried to revive the Klan by starting up a small group which he named the U.S. Klans, Knights of the Ku Klux Klan. It didn't amount to much until the Supreme Court declared the end of "separate but equal." Then membership began to soar. Within four years, the U.S. Klans was claiming 15,000 members. It was a poorly run organization and soon fell apart. But by then it hardly mattered. Many other Klan organizations had already been organized around the South, and more were springing up all the time.

In February 1960, a number of small Klans formed a coalition called the National Knights of the Ku Klux Klan. The next month, they demonstrated their new unity by setting more than 1,000 crosses ablaze across several southern states.[3]

Meanwhile, a onetime imperial wizard of the U.S. Klans named Robert Davidson had defected to form the Invisible Empire, Knights of the Ku Klux Klan of America, Inc.—or UKA for short. Around the same time, Robert Shelton, who had once been an officer of the Alabama chapter of the U.S. Klans, was forming his own organization called the Alabama Knights of the Ku Klux Klan. Shelton was a good organizer, and the Alabama Knights was soon a serious rival to both the National Knights and the UKA.

On July 8, 1961, the UKA and the Alabama Knights merged, with Shelton as the new organization's Imperial Wizard. The united group, which kept the name UKA, was then the largest Klan in the country. By the mid-1960s, it claimed the loyalty of over 30,000 white supremacists, mostly in the South.[4] The National Knights was a distant second, with about 8,000 members.

All the new Klans put together never approached the size of the Klan of the 1920s. At most, membership probably never got much above 50,000. And, unlike that of Simmons's Klan, it was almost entirely in the South. In all its many versions, this new Ku Klux Klan was primarily a response to the civil rights movement. It was an outlet for the fear, anger, and bewilderment many white southerners felt at the growing threat to Jim Crow. But, although the new Ku Klux Klan was smaller, it was even more violent than the 1920s Klan had been. In that way, it was more like the Reconstruction Klan than it was like Simmons's organization.

WAVE OF TERROR

Throughout the late 1950s and 1960s, white supremacists conducted a campaign of terror across the South. Their aim— to the extent they had any purpose beyond expressing their outrage—was to hold back the tide of integration. They hoped to frighten black people in the South into giving up their demands for civil rights. Failing that, they hoped to convince the federal government that ending legal segregation would cause more trouble than it was worth.

Many of their crimes were directed against people involved in the civil rights movement or sympathetic to it. Others were more or less random, directed against anyone who happened to be black. Almost everywhere, this campaign was spearheaded by members and sympathizers of the Ku Klux Klan.

The following are just a few of more than 1,000 possible examples of Klan and Klan-inspired violence:

In 1957, four Klansmen in South Carolina brutally beat a black man who was looking after several white children while their mother was sick.

In 1960, in Houston, a group of four thugs carved the letters "KKK" into the skin of a young man's chest.

In 1961, a Klan-led mob attacked a busload of civil rights workers—known as Freedom Riders—in Montgomery, Alabama. Besides injuring several Freedom Riders, the mob turned on reporters and photographers covering the event. Because the Montgomery authorities wouldn't protect the Freedom Riders, U.S. Attorney General Robert Kennedy was forced to send federal marshals to the city.

In 1963, a Klan sympathizer shot and killed a black civil rights leader named Medger Evers in front of his home in Jackson, Mississippi.

In 1964, several carloads of white men stopped a car carrying three young civil rights workers—two white and one black—

near the town of Philadelphia, Mississippi. The white men shot the three young men to death, set fire to their car, and buried both their bodies and the car. The killers were members of a particularly vicious Klan group known as the White Knights of Mississippi. Some of them were also local law enforcement officers.

Klan bombings were carried out all over the South. Three different black churches were bombed in Birmingham, Alabama, in the month of January 1962 alone. In September 1963, Birmingham was the scene of the single worst act of Klan violence in the 1960s. On the fifteenth of that month, a dynamite bomb went off in the 16th Street Baptist Church, killing four little girls who were there for Sunday school. In a tragic aftermath to the killings, a riot broke out in which two young boys, both black, were shot to death. Fourteen years later, a Klansman was convicted for the bombing.

THE DEFEAT OF THE KLAN

Prompted by public outrage at the Klan's violence, the federal government went on the attack against the Klan in the mid-1960s. In 1965, President Lyndon Johnson called for an investigation into the Klan. A courageous congressman from Georgia named Charles Weltner responded with hearings of his subcommittee of the House Un-American Activities Committee.

Unlike the congressional investigation of the Klan in 1921, this one produced solid results. The committee's report, issued late in 1967, exposed many of the Klan's terrorist activities and gave evidence of financial crimes as well. Much as in the 1920s, some Klan officials had been using Klan money to enrich themselves.

Seven high-ranking Klan officials, including Imperial Wizard Robert Shelton, were indicted for contempt of Congress when they refused to produce documents the House committee demanded to see. Shelton and two of the UKA's Grand Dragons were sent to prison.

The FBI infiltrated the Klan with undercover agents and informers. Some of these agents rose to positions of authority in various Klan organizations. Using the inside information they provided, the government was able to put a clamp on some of the Klan's more extreme activities.

One of the most important factors in the fight against the Klan was the growing willingness of southern juries—even white southern juries—to send Klan members to jail for their crimes. In the past, Klan members in the deep South had usually been safe from punishment. White juries were reluctant to convict them: either because they were personally sympathetic to the Klan, or because they were afraid of it. By the mid-1960s, however, that attitude was beginning to change.

The change was signaled in December 1965, when a jury in Montgomery, Alabama, convicted three Klansmen of the murder of a white civil rights worker named Viola Liuzzo. President Lyndon Johnson spoke for many other Americans, white and black, north and south, when he announced: "The whole nation can take heart that there are those in the South who believe in justice in racial matters."[5]

By the early 1970s, most Americans, even white Americans in the South, recognized the Klan for what it was. More important, they realized that the Klan had lost its desperate struggle to keep legal segregation in the South.

WHY THE KLAN FAILED TO SAVE JIM CROW

In hindsight, it seems that the Klan's campaign was doomed to fail from the start. Black people were braver, and more determined, than the Klan imagined. They would not give up their demands out of fear. And the federal government, once it was committed to ending segregation, was not about to back down to an organization like the Ku Klux Klan.

The most important reason the Klan failed was that it had totally misunderstood the American character. Its campaign of violence had the opposite effect from the one the Klan intended. The Klan members apparently believed that their terrorism would convince the rest of America that white southerners were serious in their opposition to integregation. They never seemed to realize that seeing innocent people beaten and killed would not dishearten Americans nearly as much as it would enrage them.

From the start, the Klan underestimated the moral force of the argument for civil rights. It never understood how deeply the ideals of equality and freedom were imbedded in the

Viola Liuzzo, a thirty-nine-year-old Detroit woman who was murdered by Klansmen in Alabama in March 1965. The conviction of her killers would signal a change in the attitude of white juries in the South toward Klan violence. AP/WIDE WORLD

consciousness of most Americans. Once the issue of segregation was brought to the forefront of public attention, the force of that ideal was too strong to resist. Segregation was wrong, and deep down, most Americans recognized that it was wrong. Once the question was asked directly—"Should black people be denied their basic freedoms as American citizens?"—most Americans were bound to answer, "No."

THE KLAN GAINS A FOOTHOLD IN THE NORTH

Jim Crow was dead, but racism wasn't. And neither was the Ku Klux Klan. This time, the Klan didn't disappear, even temporarily.

Klan membership *did* drop dramatically, from about 50,000 in the mid-1960s to around 1,500 in the early 1970s. But that turned out to be the low point. In the 1970s, growing racial tensions set membership climbing again. What's more, it sent it spreading into the North.

Schools in the South had been segregated by law, but schools in many northern cities had been segregated, too—not by law, but by geography. Which school a child attended depended on which neighborhood he or she lived in. Since whites lived in certain neighborhoods and blacks in others, many northern schools were either mostly white or mostly black. Some were all white or all black. Since whites controlled most of the funds that went to all the schools, in practice this usually meant that the greatest resources went to the white schools. In the North, too, schools were often separate and so "inherently unequal."

In the early 1970s, courts began ordering that students in some cities be bused to schools out of their neighborhoods. The purpose was to integrate schools that had previously been almost exclusively either white or black.

Many parents, including some black parents, were angered by busing. Some parents were sincerely worried about the quality of schooling their children would receive or about the dangers of busing them into the racially tense atmosphere of a newly integrated school. But the most violent resistance to busing came from white racists who were simply outraged that their children would be forced to go to school with black children.

In some northern cities, white parents reacted to busing the way southern whites had reacted to forced integration a decade earlier. They threw stones at the school buses. They gathered at school doorways to shout racial insults at black children or even to attack them physically. The worst violence in the North occurred in the cities of Detroit and Boston.

The tensions caused by busing and other factors led to a spurt in Klan membership during the mid- and late 1970s. By the early 1980s, the Anti-Defamation League of B'nai B'rith— a Jewish organization that keeps track of racist activity—was estimating the Klans' nationwide membership at over 10,000. More significant than the increase in sheer numbers was the fact that many of those new members were in the North. For the first time since the 1920s, the Klan was gaining a solid foothold outside the old Confederacy. Today, the biggest of all the Klans has its national headquarters in Connecticut.

THE KLAN TODAY

Altogether, more than fifty different Klan groups operate in the United States today. The largest of these is the Invisible Empire, Knights of the Ku Klux Klan, which probably has about 2,000 members nationwide. During the late 1970s and early 1980s, the Invisible Empire was second only to Robert Shelton's now-bankrupt UKA in size and power.

During those years, the KKKK was headed by one of the most flamboyant of all the Klan's Imperial Wizards, Bill Wilkinson. Under Wilkinson, the Klan remained bitterly opposed to integration of every kind—particularly integration of the schools. Much of its anger was focused on the U.S. government. It was the government, as a Klan leader named Bill Riccio complained, that "put black apes in our high schools and elementary schools with our precious superior white children and forced them to mix."[6]

"We are on the move," a Klan poster announced, "TO SEND THE GOVERNMENT IN WASHINGTON A MESSAGE. The message is simply that the white majority is fed up with federal controls over jobs, schools and virtually every facet of our lives."[7] As always, however, the Klan's deepest fear was sexual relations between the races. "We will not tolerate race-mixing," Riccio insisted. "We will not stand for it."[8]

Preparing for the "inevitable race war," Klan members receive survivalist paramilitary training in the woods near Nashville, Tennessee, in 1980. Camps like this one were sponsored by a variety of hate groups in the 1980s. COPYRIGHT ROBERT DUNNAVANT, AP/WIDE WORLD

Wilkinson was one of a new breed of postintegration Klan leaders who began talking about white people as a kind of oppressed majority. Turning the civil rights movement—and reality—upside down, he announced the founding of "a civil-rights movement for white people."[9] This idea, that it is some-how the majority and not the minority that is discriminated against, became a standard complaint within the hate move-ment in the 1980s. Now, in the early 1990s, this refrain is beginning to be heard more and more outside the hate move-ment as well.

Wilkinson brought fresh attention to the Invisible Empire by staging angry confrontations with blacks and civil rights activ-ists. The most violent took place in Decatur, Alabama, in May

1979. Four people—two white and two black—were shot. Ten Klansmen were indicted for federal crimes as a result. Ironically, Wilkinson eventually lost his leadership of the Invisible Empire after it was revealed that he had fed information about the Klan to the FBI.

Today, the Invisible Empire is unusual among the Klans in at least two ways. First, it has several klaverns outside the South, including a small one in Shelton, Connecticut, where it has its headquarters. It also claims members in Ohio, California, New York, Illinois, Maryland, Michigan, and Arizona, as well as in several southern states. And second, its imperial wizard is a northern Roman Catholic named James Farrands.

The choice of Farrands as a Klan leader was met with horror by most Catholics who heard of it. The United States Catholic Conference responded by calling on every Catholic to "proclaim to all that the sin of racism defiles the image of God and degrades the sacred dignity of humankind."[10]

Farrands is less extreme in his racist proclamations than some of the more radical Klan leaders. Claiming to be a fighter against drugs, crime, and unemployment, he sometimes sounds more like a right-wing political extremist than an old-style Klansman. And he has, in fact, tried to rally Klan support around right-wing political candidates.[11]

The only other Klan organization that can claim to be national, in the sense that it has klaverns in several states, is the Knights of the Ku Klux Klan. Led in the 1970s by David Duke, an ex-Nazi who is now a state representative in Louisiana, the KKKK is presently split into two main factions. The smaller of the two, with only about 250 members, is headed by another ex-Nazi named Don Black. Black lost control of the rest of the KKKK in 1982, when he was sent to federal prison for two years. The larger faction, which has 500 to 750 members, is headed by Stanley McCollum and located in Tuscumbia, Alabama. It publishes the Klan's best-known newspaper, *The White Patriot*. (This is not to be confused with the White Patriot party, a separate Klan group, or with the Christian Patriots, another kind of hate group altogether.) One of the most notable of the KKKK klaverns is located in the Chicago, Illinois, area.

Most of the other Klans are small, local organizations that operate independently of any larger group. The best known of these is probably the Christian Knights of the KKK. Although the Christian Knights has only about 200 to 250 members, most of whom are in North Carolina, it is one of the most visible and publicity-hungry of all the Klans. This group is led by Virgil Griffin, whose specialty is staging small Klan marches that generate large amounts of attention. Griffin himself was among several white supremacists who went to Greensboro, North Carolina, to violently attack a left-wing anti-Klan rally on November 3, 1979. Five anti-Klan demonstrators were shot dead in the attack.

Among the few independent Klans outside the South are the Ohio Knights, the White Unity party (in Pennsylvania), the Invisible Empire Knights (in New Jersey), the American Knights (in California), and the White Knights of the Ku Klux Klan (in New York).

Total membership in all the Klans combined currently amounts to less than 6,000. That's a drop of almost half since the early 1980s. But the relatively low numbers are misleading. For every Klan member, there are probably between five and ten active Klan sympathizers: people who attend Klan demonstrations or participate in other Klan-led activities. In addition, there are probably many others who are influenced by Klan propaganda.

Most important of all, the Klan is no longer virtually alone as America's only significant white supremacy organization. Many other equally bigoted and equally violent hate groups have risen up in recent decades. Membership in the Klan may have declined, but membership in these newer hate groups has risen even more.

6

The Ghost of Adolf Hitler: America's Neo-Nazis

Several American hate groups take their inspiration from Adolf Hitler and the National Socialist (Nazi) party that took over Germany in the 1930s. The most overwhelmingly destructive hate group in history, the German Nazis led the world into World War II, deliberately murdered millions of people, and left not only Germany but most of Europe in ruins.

The Nazis' philosophy, which today's so-called neo-Nazis admire, was a combination of racism and military ambition. The Nazis believed that "pure" Germans were "Aryans," descendants of the nomadic tribes that had conquered India around 1500 B.C. They believed that virtually everything worthwhile—in art and learning, science and technology—was the "creative product" of peoples descended from these tribes.

Even a quick reading of world history shows that the Nazis' claims for the Aryan race are false. All kinds of people have made great contributions to science, art, and technology. Both writing and mathematics, for instance, were first developed by Arabs. There were flowering civilizations in Africa before any of those in Europe. Cultures all over the world have produced great works of art. And no country ever produced more technological inventions than the United States, probably the most racially and ethnically mixed nation in history.

In recent years, biologists and other scientists have come to understand that race is not an important factor in the differences between individual people. Some have come to question whether "race" has any scientific significance at all. As Robert Moore, a prominent sociologist from King's College in Aberdeen has said, "most social scientists regard scientific racism as dead."[1] In the 1920s and 1930s, however, many scientists formulated racist theories that seemed to support the Nazis' belief that all other races were inferior to their "master race." Like modern white supremacists in the United States, the Nazis believed that it was vital for them to avoid mixing their blood with other races, particularly the Jewish race.

The Nazis were viciously anti-Semitic. That is, they had a bitter hatred for the Jews. Although the Nazis insisted that the Jews were an inferior race, they gave them credit for enormous power. Hitler blamed the Jews for Germany's defeat in World War I. He believed that Jews controlled international finance and were secretly allied with the Communists to control the world. Since the Nazis wanted to control the world themselves, this made them special enemies.

The Nazis believed in strict obedience to a leader—or Führer. That leader was Adolf Hitler, who became chancellor of Germany in 1933. Once in office, he seized dictatorial power and turned Germany into a totalitarian state. Everything was put under government—that is, Nazi—control. All other political parties were banned. Labor unions were outlawed. Even books, paintings, plays, and movies the Nazis didn't like were banned. The secret police, known as the Gestapo, ruthlessly crushed any potential political opposition. The image of the swastika, the twisted cross that is the Nazi symbol, was everywhere.

Much of the Nazis' appeal was based on a glorification of brute force and violence. Even before they came to power, the Nazis had their own militia, uniformed roughnecks who strode through the streets beating up people who opposed them. Once in power, they had the SS, a special branch of the military that soon became notorious for its merciless cruelty. Within a few years of Hitler's taking office, he had made the German military the most powerful in the world. He boasted that he was building a "Thousand Year Reich": a Nazi state that would last for a thousand years.

In 1939, Hitler launched a campaign of military conquest that plunged the world into war. Before they were finally defeated in 1945, the Nazis managed to take control of most of Europe. In Germany, they had ruthlessly persecuted the Jews and other minorities. Under the Nuremburg Laws of 1935, for example, Jews were denied all legal rights. They were forbidden to marry non-Jews and to work in certain important professions. The government took their property. Many Jews fled the country. Those who stayed were soon rounded up and sent to extermination camps.

The German Jews were joined in those camps by millions of other Jews from nations conquered by the Nazis, along with millions of others—communists, gypsies, liberals, and everyone else the Nazis considered their enemies. Most of them were systematically killed. Estimates of the number of European Jews murdered by the Nazis range from 5 million to over 6 million. Altogether, the Nazis murdered between 9 million and 10 million people in the slaughter that became known as the Holocaust. And that does not even include those who died in battle.

The Nazi dream of glory turned out to be a nightmare. Within a few years, the Allies, led by the United States, Great Britain, and the Soviet Union, defeated Nazi Germany. It surrendered on May 7, 1945. Hitler had already killed himself in his underground hideout a week before.

The Nazi experiment was a terrible failure. The "Thousand Year Reich" had lasted only a decade. In that short time, the Nazis not only had destroyed themselves, but had brought about the most massive tragedy in human history. All told, some 55 million men, women, and children died in the war the Nazis had started. More than 400,000 of them were Americans. Over half of the dead—roughly 30 million innocent human beings—were civilians.

With this disastrous example before them, it seems absurd that anyone would want to follow in the Nazis' footsteps. And yet, American neo-Nazis regard Hitler as a hero. They look to him and his ideas for inspiration, and they have taken his love of violence and hatred of other races as their own.

THE AMERICAN NAZI PARTY

In the 1930s, before Germany's attempt to conquer Europe, Hitler had many admirers in the United States. Among them were thousands of German-Americans who supported the Nazis out of loyalty to their old homeland. Some of these were organized into groups called German-American Bunds.

Most of these prewar sympathizers abandoned their admiration for the Nazis when the United States went to war with Germany. Almost all reacted with horror when they found out the full extent of the Nazis' atrocities. Some, however, did not. One was a young man named George Lincoln Rockwell, who founded the American Nazi party only a few years after the war. Its headquarters were in Arlington, Virginia, near the largest U.S. military cemetery, where thousands of Americans killed fighting the German Nazis are buried.

The American Nazis based their party openly on the German model. They wore military uniforms that aped the ones the German Nazis had worn. Rockwell's Arlington headquarters was filled with swastikas and photographs of Hitler. Rockwell seemed to think of himself as a kind of American Hitler. He even posed for pictures below a large cutout of a swastika, with a globe of the earth entrapped in its center.

Rockwell preached the same racist philosophy that Hitler had preached. He wanted to deal with non-Aryan minorities in much the same way his idol had. "We believe that Adolf Hitler was the gift of an inscrutable Providence to a world on the brink of a Jewish-Bolshevik catastrophe," he wrote. "Only the blazing sprit of this heroic man can give us . . . strength and inspiration."[2] Most Jews, Rockwell said, would have to be killed. As for the millions of black Americans, they could simply be sent "back" to Africa.

Rockwell became a well-known figure, speaking on college campuses and elsewhere around the country, but he never attracted large numbers of people to his group. After he was assassinated in August 1967 by a fellow Nazi, his small party was further split by internal power struggles. But, as small and

The would-be American Hitler—George Lincoln Rockwell, the founder of the American Nazi party—holding a press conference at party headquarters in 1965. The man on the left is Matt Koehl, who would carry on after Rockwell was assassinated two years later. AP/WIDE WORLD

ineffective as it was, it provided a model and an inspiration for several other hate groups that would grow up in its wake.

THE DESCENDANTS OF GEORGE LINCOLN ROCKWELL

Some of Rockwell's own followers went on to lead their own neo- (or new) Nazi groups after his death. Two of them are still significant forces in the Nazi movement today.

Matt Koehl took over the reins of the original American Nazi party, renaming it the National Socialist White People's party. Among its goals, as spelled out in Koehl's propaganda sheet *White Power,* were a clean environment, an "end to economic free-loading" by rich and poor alike, "white self-defense," and promotion of "an Aryan culture." Most of all, "an all-White

America without swarming racial aliens," and "White World Solidarity," in which the "white" nations of the world would presumably join together to fend off the advancement of the colored nations. Koehl didn't consider his racist beliefs to be personal prejudices. He regarded them as a spiritual faith, and called "betterment" of the "white race" a "sacred task."[3]

In the 1980s, Koehl renamed the party the New Order and moved its headquarters to New Berlin, a town of about 30,000, not far from Milwaukee, Wisconsin. He is attempting to build a white, neo-Nazi settlement called Nordland in rural Wisconsin. He hopes to use it as "a base for the future growth and expansion" of the National Socialist movement. If so, he has a long way to go. In 1988, the Anti-Defamation League estimated that the New Order had a total of roughly 100 dues-paying members, and there is no indication that it has grown much since.[4]

The second ex-Rockwell assistant still active is William Pierce. Pierce had been an assistant professor of physics at the University of Oregon before leaving to join Rockwell and the American Nazi party. A writer, he edited the party's journal, *The National Socialist World*. After Rockwell's death, Pierce split with Koehl. He set up an entirely new organization called Youth for Wallace to drum up support for the white supremacist governor of Alabama, George Wallace, who was then running for president.

Youth for Wallace also served as a recruiting ground for Pierce's neo-Nazi movement. Once the election was over, he renamed the group he'd formed the National Youth Alliance. For a while, his fellow leader in the NYA was Willis Carto, who would later become well known in right-wing political circles as head of the so-called Liberty Lobby. Eventually, however, Pierce took sole personal control of the NYA, renaming it the National Alliance, and establishing its headquarters in West Virginia. He still runs it today, along with something called the Cosmotheist Church. He claims that the church is a religious organization, but the IRS moved to take away its tax-exempt status in 1983, pointing out that it called for violence against minorities.[5] Although Pierce does not emphasize his groups' origins in the old-line Nazi movement, his ideas are clearly based on the Nazi tradition.

Pierce's influence goes far beyond his own small organizations. He is one of the leading propagandists for white supremacy, and the National Alliance is a major source of hate group literature. In addition to its own bimonthly sheet, *The National Vanguard,* it distributes a number of racist magazines, flyers, and books.

Under the pen name Andrew MacDonald, Pierce is the author of *The Turner Diaries,* an influential 1974 novel that gives a glorified account of a future (1990s) world revolution carried out by a neo-Nazi-style guerrilla group called the Order. Starting with more or less ordinary terrorist tactics, the Order proceeds to armed attacks on government buildings and finally the use of atomic weapons. Before the book is over, the Order has succeeded in wiping out every Jew in the world.[6]

Although it is a work of fiction, the NA considers the book a "handbook for white victory."[7] Although the story it tells is unlikely, it does seem to have provided a model for a band of would-be revolutionaries who also called themselves the Order.

THE ORDER

Also known as the Silent Brotherhood, the real-life Order was founded in October 1983 by a follower of William Pierce named Robert Mathews. Mathews seems to have gotten the idea for his organization partly from the *Diaries* and partly from a 1970s band of armed fanatics who called themselves the Minutemen.[8]

Mathews and a dozen or so companions swore a chilling oath: "I, as a free Aryan man, hereby swear an unrelenting oath upon the green graves of our sires, upon the children in the wombs of our wives, upon the throne of God almighty . . . to join together in holy union with those brothers in this circle and to declare forthright that from this moment on I have no fear of death, no fear of foe: that I have a sacred duty to do whatever is necessary to deliver our people from the Jew and bring total victory to the Aryan race."[9]

What was "necessary," according to the Order, was a terrorist war against the government of the United States. On November 24, 1984, Mathews and his comrades signed a secret document declaring that "from this day forward, we no longer consider the regime in Washington to be a valid and lawful representative of all Aryans who refuse to submit to the coercion and subtle tyranny placed upon us by Tel Aviv and their lackeys in Washington. . . . This is war!"[10] The belief that the U.S. government is somehow controlled by the Jews in Israel is common among neo-Nazis. They often refer to the U.S. government as ZOG, short for Zionist Occupied Government.

For more than a year after their declaration of war, Mathews and his friends went on a rampage of crime and terror that included bombings, robberies, and arsons, as well as cold-blooded murder. Some of their crimes were spectacular enough to grab national attention. One of them was the murder of the popular radio talk show host Alan Berg. Another was a daring daylight robbery of a Brinks armored car on an entrance ramp to Highway 20 near Ukiah, California. Led by Robert Mathews, the robbers escaped in two pickup trucks with around $3.8 million, the most ever stolen in an armored-car robbery in American history. This money, along with the loot from other robberies, was intended to support the white supremacy movement and finance the hoped-for white revolution.

The attention the Order's crimes attracted eventually led to the group's downfall. Federal law enforcement agencies targeted the terrorists and quickly brought most of them to trial. In 1985, twenty-four Order members were charged with racketeering. All either pled guilty or were convicted. Several got prison sentences of from 40 to 100 years. Some Order members were also convicted of other crimes, including the murder of Alan Berg.

Bob Mathews himself was killed in a shootout with the FBI and a police SWAT team. Pinned down in a hideout on an island near Portland, Oregon, he refused to come out even after flares were shot through the windows and the house caught on fire.[11]

Although the Order was crushed, most of the money it stole was never found. One captured Order member claimed that much of the money had been distributed to various leaders of the hate movement, including William Pierce. The informant later denied his statement. But some of the money, at least, had been distributed because one movement figure, Dan Gayman, eventually returned $15,000 he got from Mathews and another Order member.[12]

7

A Case of Mistaken Identity: Confusing Hatred with Religion

Christianity grew out of the traditions of the Jewish religion. The Old Testament of the Christian Bible is, in essence, a Jewish document. Jesus Christ himself was born a Jew. Yet, in spite of all this, many Christians are anti-Semitic, or anti-Jew. All of the major hate groups are anti-Semitic to some extent, but none are more viciously hostile to Jews than those that are part of the so-called Christian Identity movement.

THE ORIGINS OF CHRISTIAN IDENTITY

Christian Identity traces its beliefs back to a small religious sect that sprang up in England around the middle of the nineteenth century. That sect was founded by a minister named John Wilson, who based its beliefs on his own peculiar reading of a short passage in the Old Testament. The passage mentions a bow and arrow that belonged to a distant ancestor of Jesus Christ named Joseph. Joseph was the son of Jacob, also known as Israel. Since the English bowmen of the Middle Ages were said to be the best in the world, Wilson decided the passage meant that the English were the real descendants of Jacob, the blood relatives of Jesus Christ. In Wilson's strange logic, that meant that the English were the *real* Israelites—the real descendants of Israel—and therefore God's chosen people. And that, in turn, meant that the Jews were imposters.

Wilson's eccentric ideas were brought to America by the Reverend Edward Hine in the 1880s. Hine was convinced that the United States was destined to be "the new Jerusalem," the second homeland of the real Israelites. In England, Wilson's religion was known as Anglo-Israelism or British Israelism. In the United States, it came to be known as Christian Identity. Today, Christian Identity is not so much a single religion as a collection of small groups sharing similar beliefs.

Many of Hine's teachings were eventually embraced by a twentieth-century American anti-Semite named Gerald L. K. Smith, the leader of the Christian Nationalist Crusade in the 1930s. He also spread his anti-Semitic doctrine through a journal called *The Cross and the Flag*. After his death, the "Crusade" was carried on by Smith's equally anti-Semitic (and anti-Catholic, and anti-black) lieutenant, Wesley Swift.

By the 1960s, the Identity movement was centered in California, where Swift had a church. Swift was a blatant racist, who made segregation a religious duty. "If you believe the Bible," he wrote, "you are going to be a segregationist."[1] Although he called himself a Christian minister, he sounded more like a follower of Adolf Hitler than of Jesus Christ, telling his congregation that "all Jews must be destroyed."[2] He bitterly attacked all non-Identity ministers and priests as "stooges" and "Anti-Christs in the pulpit."[3]

TOPSY-TURVY

How can people who call themselves Christians hate the Jews when Christ himself was Jewish? In the case of Christian Identity followers, they do it by denying several realities that are understood and accepted by almost everyone else.

In the topsy-turvy world of Christian Identity, everything is upside down or backward. Christ's ancestors were not Jews, nor are the people everyone else considers Jews today. The real Jews, according to the followers of Christian Identity, are white American Christians of British descent. As an Identity follower wrote in the publication *Christian Vanguard*, "It is utterly sinful to call Christ 'Jewish'." The whole idea of a Biblical connection between Judaism and Christianity is "a diabolical farce. . . . There is NO common-ness between us and Jewry."[4]

If the Jews aren't Jews, then who are they? According to Identity, they are actually the cursed children of Satan—the descendants of Cain, who killed his brother Abel. What's more, according to Identity's strange racial distinctions, Jews are not even white.

Identity followers deny modern, as well as biblical, history. They are convinced, for example, that the Nazi slaughter of European Jews never took place. They admit that *some* Jews were *probably* killed, but not very many. The Holocaust was a fiction invented by the same international Jewish conspiracy they insist controls the world's media and international finance. In order to believe all this, Identity followers have to ignore an enormous amount of evidence. It includes not only the physical evidence of the Nazi death camps, but the testimony of thousands of survivors and of the Allied soldiers who liberated them at the end of the war.

While they stubbornly ignore such solid evidence, Identity followers seem ready to accept any claim that supports their anti-Semitic prejudices, no matter how flimsy. A good example is *The Protocols of the Learned Elders of Zion,* a book that pretends to be a secret Jewish blueprint for dominating the world. Identity followers insist that this document is real, even though it is well known as a forgery produced by the Russian czar's secret police almost a century ago.[5]

Christian Identity followers look down on the non-white races. According to Identity "theology," only white Anglo-Saxon Aryans are really human beings at all. All the other peoples on earth are pre-Adamic.[6] That is, more primitive creatures whose ancestors date from before the moment God created human beings. Identity followers refer to them collectively as "mud people."

Eventually, Identity followers believe, the world will be destroyed in a great war to the death between the whites and the "mud people." Some Identity groups have built survivalist camps, where they give their members military-style training to enable them to survive and win this "inevitable" conflict. Other white supremacists run similar camps. Bill Wilkinson's Klan group, for example, once had a camp called My Lai, after the village where American troops killed 347 Vietnamese civilians in 1968.[7] In 1985, the FBI identified sixteen such camps in states around the country.

The first Identity group to grab national attention was the Posse Comitatus. The Posse combines the racial and religious views of the Christian Identity movement with some equally eccentric political and financial theories of its own.

Posse members insist that the United States is a "Christian Republic." The only law they recognize is what they call "Christian Common Law," which is based on their reading of the Bible. They reject all the laws passed by the federal and state governments. In fact, they deny the authority of those levels of government altogether, claiming that the only legitimate legal authority rests at the county level. *Posse Comitatus* means "power of the county" in Latin.

Among other things, the Posse rejects the government's role in the printing of currency. It insists that gold and silver are the only valid forms of money and that charging interest for money is a sin. Devoted Posse members often refuse to pay income taxes, occasionally bringing them into conflict with law enforcement agencies. Since many Posse members are gun-toting survivalists, these clashes have sometimes turned violent.

As its name suggests, the Posse consists largely of small, more or less local bands. The first of these was organized in Portland, Oregon, by Henry (Mike) Beach, an ex-member of a Nazi-sympathizing group known as the Silver Shirts.[8] The most influential of the early Posse groups was a California chapter founded by William Potter Gale, a retired army colonel. Gale was an associate of Wesley Swift's who presided over his own Identity church in Mariposa, California.

The Posse first came to public attention in the late 1970s and early 1980s. At that time, an economic crisis was sweeping rural America and the value of American farmland was plummeting. Many small farmers were caught with large mortgages on land no longer worth as much as they still owed on it. Since crop prices were falling, too, many could not possibly pay their taxes, much less keep up their mortgages. A lot of them lost their farms altogether. In some cases, the government claimed the land and auctioned off the farmers' property to pay the taxes.

The Posse launched a drive to enlist troubled farmers in its cause. It told them that the banks had no right to charge them interest on their mortgages. Their troubles were all caused by a plot by an international conspiracy of Jews and bankers to steal Christian land.

The Posse's antibank, antitax, antigovernment stand appealed to some desperate farmers facing bankruptcy and debt. The Posse held out a cruel, false hope to them. It told them that they might save their farms by refusing to cooperate with the tax collectors. Instead of saving their farms, however, the Posse's schemes only got many farmers in trouble with the law.

The farm crisis established the Posse as a rural, farm-based movement. By 1976, the FBI was reporting that there were at least seventy-eight Posse chapters in twenty-three states. According to an FBI report, most of the Posse's members were "rural people."[9]

By the early 1980s, the Posse Comitatus had become extremely militant. In 1982, a Posse radio broadcast was calling on members to prepare for battle. "You'd better start making dossiers, names, addresses, phone numbers, car license plate numbers, on every damn Jew rabbi in this land, and every Anti-Defamation League leader or JDL [Jewish Defense League] leader in this land, and you better start doing it now. And know where he is. If you have to be told any more than that, you're too damn dumb to bother with. You get these road block locations, where you can set up ambushes, and get it all working now."[10]

POSSE VIOLENCE

In August 1985, Nebraska State Patrol officers raided a farm near the small town of Rulo. It belonged to Michael Ryan, who used it as the headquarters of a particularly mysterious Posse chapter. The police had been to Ryan's farm before and found a large stash of guns, ammunition, and paramilitary survival gear. This time they found worse: the buried bodies of a twenty-six-year-old man and a five-year-old child. Both had been members of Ryan's Posse cult, and both had been tortured before they died. Ryan and his grown son were eventually found guilty of the murders. Among their possessions was Posse propaganda telling the story of Gordon Kahl.[11]

Kahl was the Posse's most prominent hero and martyr. At the time of his death in 1983, he was a sixty-three-year-old North Dakota farmer and Posse organizer. In the 1970s, he had served time in federal prison for refusing to pay his income taxes. In February 1983, federal marshals stopped Kahl, his son, and another Posse member along a rural highway in North Dakota. They wanted to arrest Gordon for a parole violation. But Kahl had sworn never to go back to prison, and he meant it.

Like many other Posse members, Kahl and his companions were survivalists. They went armed, and they considered it their right to defend themselves from the agents of the "illegal" U.S. government. Opening fire on the law officers, they killed two of them and wounded three others. Kahl's son was also wounded in the shootout, but all the Posse members managed to escape.

The law finally caught up with Gordon Kahl on June 3, 1983, at the home of another Posse member near Smithville, Arkansas. Once again, Kahl resisted. He was killed in a one-on-one gunfight with a brave county sheriff named Gene Mathews, who had managed to enter the house. Mathews was killed as well.[12] Kahl was killed in a shootout with a representative of the only level of government the Posse is willing to recognize.

THE POSSE TODAY

In the mid-1980s, a Posse group led by James Wickstrom tried to found its own country government near the little town of Tigerton, Wisconsin. The state refused to recognize the Posse's county, and the heavily armed Posse encampment refused to acknowledge the state's authority. For a time, there was a standoff, and fear of a pitched battle, but eventually the authorities moved in, and the Posse group gave up. Wickstrom, who by then was considered the Posse's national leader, was convicted of impersonating a public official and sent to jail. When he got out, he left Wisconsin and moved to Pennsylvania, where he apparently intended to set up a survivalist camp. By

The hero and martyr of the Posse Comitatus movement, Gordon Kahl. AP/
WIDE WORLD

1988, he was in trouble again, faced with charges involving counterfeiting and a plot to buy stolen weapons. He was freed after a mistrial.[13]

Posse members apparently continue to come up with schemes that violate or ignore various financial laws. According to Klanwatch, an organization that keeps track of all kinds of white supremacist activity, four suspected Posse members were arrested for involvement in an illegal $3 million real estate deal in 1989.

It is impossible to tell how many Posse Comitatus groups are active today. There is no central Posse organization, and individual Posse chapters often operate in secret. What's more, it's difficult to tell the difference between an actual Posse chapter and one of many similar local-based hate groups. But in 1985, Leonard Zeskind, of the antihate-group Center for Democratic Renewal, estimated that the "racist and anti-Semitic movement" had somewhere between 2,000 and 5,000 activist members in the American farm belt. And for each of them, he estimated, there were probably seven to ten sympathizers.[14]

THE CHRISTIAN PATRIOTS

In 1959, a millionaire named John R. Harrell established the Christian Conservative Churches of America. They would, he declared, combine "Christianity and Patriotism" to fight "Zionism and Communism." (Zionism was the movement that established a Jewish state in Palestine. Anti-Semites use the word to refer to the supposed Jewish conspiracy to control the world.) In 1977, Harrell went on to found a survivalist group called the Christian Patriots Defense League, and his movement soon came to be known as the Christian Patriots.

Like many other right-wing Americans, the Christian Patriots believe that the government has too much power over the lives of its citizens. But the Patriots go much further than most conservatives. They don't just object to paying high income taxes, they object to having any income taxes at all. They even object to driver's and marriage licenses. Among the things opposed by the Christian Patriots are "humanism, modernism, communism, regionalism, Judaism, integration," and of course, the government confiscation of guns.[15]

The most extreme Christian Patriots are convinced that "niggers and Jews" are out to destroy the "Caucasian race." Like other Identity-style groups, they are convinced that society is doomed to explode into a great race war, with the other races attacking the white people to take their last possessions from them. Many are determined to prepare for the final battle they believe will take place in what Harrell has described as "the New JerUSAlem, the United States of America."[16] "Buy yourselves a gun," Harrell once told a gathering of the United Klans of America, "and then buy some ammunition. If you don't get the ammunition, you might as well . . . beat them to death."[17]

Despite all their violent talk, the Christian Patriots have not engaged in any widespread violence. In fact, the group has forbidden members to bring weapons to their annual "Freedom Festival" in Missouri, where paramilitary training is illegal. But a 1985 incident in Seattle, Washington demonstrated where their beliefs can lead. On Christmas Eve of that year, a Seattle Patriot named Donald Rice went berserk and murdered a whole family of four people, including two children, because he'd heard that they were Jewish and communists. They weren't.[18]

THE ARYAN NATIONS

Throughout the 1980s and into the 1990s, the most prominent figure in the Identity movement has been Richard Girnt Butler. Butler is an aerospace engineer who was brought into the movement by William Potter Gale. On the strength of a correspondence course in theology, Butler was ordained a Methodist minister, and after Wesley Swift's death in 1970, he took over Swift's Anglo-Saxon Christian Congregation. Butler has been ironically referred to as "the spiritual leader of the white supremacist movement."[19]

In 1974, Butler established a large compound near the town of Hayden Lake, Idaho, which he called the Aryan Nations. He hopes to make it the heartland of a separate, all-white nation in the Pacific Northwest. As he wrote in a letter to his followers, "the five northwest states area is not the finest of the land of North America . . . nor is it a great industrial area. Yet

it is a fine land for a White (Aryan) nation resurrection."[20]
Many other white supremacists share a similar dream. They
call themselves by such names as "Christian nationalists,"
"white nationalists," or "white separatists."

The Aryan Nations was and is part hate group, part religion,
and part business. The "church" Butler runs at Hayden Lake
is called the Church of Jesus Christ Christian. Twice a week,
when Butler preaches there, he tapes his sermons to sell to
supporters around the country. He also does a brisk business
in Klan, Nazi, and Aryan Nations souvenirs and regalia on the
side.

Just how many followers Butler has isn't known. At one
point, he claimed as many as 6,000 (whom he encouraged to
send a portion of their incomes to Hayden Lake to support the
cause). Today, he claims less than a hundred members in his
regular congregation at Hayden Lake, but "several thousands"
of supporters around the country and abroad.[21]

A GATHERING OF VULTURES

The significance of the Aryan Nations goes far beyond Butler's
congregation, however big it may actually be. Hayden Lake
has become a rallying point for white supremacists of many
different kinds. Each July, the Aryan Nations compound is the
site of a gathering of white supremacists from all over the
country, representing at least thirteen different Klan and Nazi
organizations.

The most significant of the Hayden Lake meetings took
place in 1983, the year an ex-Klansman from Texas named
Louis Beam gave a rousing speech, in which he declared: "We
are at war! We must pledge our blood for the new nation!
There's nothing we won't do to bring about the new kingdom,
the new nation!"[22] At least one of Beam's listeners took him at
his word. That was Bob Mathews. A few months later he would
found the Order and begin to convert the Aryan Nations' hot
talk of fight-to-the-death revolution into reality.

THE COVENANT, THE SWORD, AND THE ARM OF THE LORD

Another person who attended the rousing World Aryan Congress meeting at Hayden Lake in 1983 was James Ellison.

The Reverend Richard Butler, preaching in his church at the Aryan Nations headquarters, Hayden Lake, Idaho, in 1984. AP/WIDE WORLD

Ellison, who called himself "King James of the Ozarks," was the quirky leader of an Identity survivalist group with the three-barreled name the Covenant, the Sword, and the Arm of the Lord. The CSA made its headquarters in a camp called Zarephath-Horeb in the Ozark mountains near the Missouri-Arkansas border. Residents of the camp received paramilitary training for the expected race war at Ellison's Endtime Overcomer Survival Training School.

In the meantime, at least a few of the students put their training to use in other ways. Some CSA members were involved in the firebombing of a Christian church and a Jewish community center. One named Richard Snell was captured by police in Oklahoma in June 1984, shortly after murdering an Arkansas state trooper. The trooper had pulled him over earlier in the day for an ordinary traffic check. It was not Snell's first crime, or even his first murder. It turned out he had also killed a pawnshop owner in Texarkana, Arkansas, seven months before. Snell's most ambitious scheme for the CSA was to blow up the main gas pipeline leading into the city of Chicago. Fortunately, it failed.[23] He was eventually sentenced to death for the killing of the pawnbroker.[24]

In April 1985, the FBI laid seige to Zarephath-Horeb. Ellison, along with other CSA members and a few Order members who happened to be there, held out for three days before he surrendered. Ellison and some of the others were charged with racketeering and other federal crimes. Like many captured criminals, Ellison quickly turned on his comrades. He cooperated with the FBI and eventually testified against fellow leaders of the Identity movement in a federal court.

Searching the CSA encampment, the FBI found thirty gallons of cyanide as well as a rocket launcher, land mines, and a variety of other illegal weapons. That amount of cyanide is enough to kill hundreds, if not thousands, of people. The authorities guessed that it had been intended to poison some city's water supply.[25]

8

New Recruits

According to the Anti-Defamation League and other sources, many older hate groups have been losing members in the past few years.[1] Several of the hate movement's traditional sources of recruits have been drying up. Rural America is no longer the rich source of members for the Klan and the Posse that it used to be; and the white South now accepts racial integration about as comfortably as any other major region of the country. But this doesn't mean that the hate movement is dying out. It may even be growing. A new breed of white supremacists has been finding ways to appeal to a whole new generation of haters.

THE LARRY KING OF THE HATE MOVEMENT

In recent years, the hate movement's most effective recruiter has been a TV repairman from Fallbrook, California, named Tom Metzger. Metzger has had ties to virtually every branch of the hate movement, including the Klan, the neo-Nazis, and Christian Identity. For some years, he has been the host of his own cable television show, called "Race and Reason," which appears on several public-access TV channels around the country.

"Race and Reason" is a talk show. On the surface, it looks a little bit like an amateurishly produced "Larry King Show," with the host, Metzger, sitting and chatting with guests. But, unlike King—or Phil Donahue, or Oprah Winfrey—Metzger has a single ideological purpose behind his show: the promotion of white supremacy. Not surprisingly, his guests tend to be fellow members of the hate movement.

Metzger has taken advantage of the laws requiring local cable companies to open up channels for programs provided by the public to get his show on several cable systems around the country. Just how many local systems is hard to say. He claims to be on "approximately fifty," but critics suspect that the real number is much lower.

The talk on "Race and Reason" is about what you'd expect from a mixed bag of white supremacists. Although some guests, and Metzger himself, do their best to sound reasonable, the show's conversation is often studded with racist hate words like "nigger" and "gook." The host's idea of humor seems to be referring to his country as the "Jew-nited States."[2]

Metzger's program is probably watched mostly by people who are already committed to the hate movement, but controversy about it has resulted in a lot of publicity in some communities. That publicity has made Metzger one of the best-known leaders in the entire white supremacy movement. He has used that recognition and his television know-how to get appearances on such national TV programs as "Donahue," "Oprah Winfrey," and "Crossfire." But Metzger's most lasting influence hasn't come through his TV show. It's come through an organization he founded called the White Aryan Resistance—or W.A.R., for short.

W.A.R.

W.A.R. is essentially a propaganda organization. "Our goal," Metzger once told Scholastic Update, "is total racial revolution. And we're prepared to use violence."[3] Beyond that, W.A.R.'s program is unclear. Although Metzger was once an Identity minister in the New Christian Crusade Church, he denies that W.A.R. promotes the Christian Identity point of view. In fact, he denies that W.A.R. promotes any ideology at all.

"We are not pro- or anti-Christian, pro- or anti-communist," Metzger insists. "White revolutionaries have no dogmas." Any point of view or "ism" seems to be okay with W.A.R., as long as it is both white and racist. "Whatever benefits white racial culture, we endorse," says Metzger. "Whatever degrades our race, we oppose."[4]

Metzger sometimes denies that he's a white supremacist at all, claiming only that he's a "white separatist." That is, he belongs to the branch of the hate movement that wants to turn five states in the Pacific Northwest into a separate, all-white nation. On at least one occasion, however, he has referred to the "white racist movement" and clearly included himself within it.[5]

GOING AFTER THE YOUNG

Some of Metzger's most successful recruiting efforts have been directed at young people. W.A.R. has had three different youth arms. The White Aryan Resistance Youth aims primarily at recruiting skinheads, members of street gangs who shave their heads and proclaim their love of violence. The Aryan Youth Movement and the White Student Union (sometimes referred to jointly as the AYM/WSU) are designed to attract more traditional and conservative young people. Despite this difference, they all seem to be essentially the same organization, with the same leadership and the same basic purpose—recruiting a new generation of haters for the white supremacy movement.

An AYM/WSU "recruitment flyer" describes the organization's purpose as the "promotion of PURE RACISM." (Racist literature is full of capitals. It's a way of shouting at the reader in print.) "We strive towards PURE RACISM because we understand it. We understand PURE RACISM because it is simple and uncomplicated and that SIMPLICITY IS GENIUS." Like W.A.R., the AYM/WSU is not fond of philosophical nit-picking. Although it claims to encourage young people to think for themselves, it discourages them from thinking too deeply about white supremacist ideology. "As White Youth, we may not fully understand the disagreements and debates between various White Power organizations," the AYM/WSU flyer admits. "Therefore, we don't care about the difference."[6]

The first head of the AYM/WSU was Greg Withrow. The

son of a friend of Tom Metzger, Withrow was raised in the hate movement. Speaking at an Aryan Nations congress at Hayden Lake, Withrow declared, "Either we shall obtain our goals peacefully or we shall take the matter to the field utilizing the revolutionary arm of young white militants. Peace is preferable. However, if our race is left no choice . . . the White Youth of this nation shall utilize every method . . . to neutralize and quite possibly engage in the wholesale extermination of all subhuman non-Aryans from the face of the North American continent; men, women, and children, without exception, without appeals, who are of non-Aryan blood shall be terminated or expelled." No one in that audience could have doubted what "terminated" meant. To lead this new society, Withrow called for "a generation of ruthless predators that shall make past Aryan leadership and warriors seem pale by comparison."[7]

Withrow eventually had a change of heart, becoming so sick on the poison of his own hatred that he left not only the AYM/WSU but the whole white supremacy movement. The hate movement, however, can be a difficult thing to leave behind. After he gave an interview to his local newspaper, the *Sacramento Bee,* he was viciously attacked by some of his former comrades. They beat him with a baseball bat, slashed his chest with a razor, and then slowly drove nails through his hands. Withrow survived. Whether out of old loyalty or new fear, he still refuses to give the names of his attackers, but he does identify them as "three former disciples" in the movement.[8]

Withrow's place as leader of AYM/WSU was taken by Tom Metzger's son John. John, now in his early twenties, is an extremely effective rabble rouser and recruiter. He and his fellow W.A.R.-riors have visited many colleges, high schools, and even some elementary schools, enlisting young followers. At one time, they claimed to have seventeen chapters in various cities around the country.

Opponents of the hate movement consider efforts like Metzger's the most frightening of all recent developments. In that one thing, they agree with the AYM/WSU recruitment bulletin that declares: "WHOEVER HAS THE YOUTH HAS THE FUTURE."[9]

Racist Skinheads

Skinheads are gangs of young toughs who ape a style that originated in England during the 1970s. The first American skinhead gang, calling itself Romantic Violence, didn't show up in Chicago until the mid-1980s, but it wasn't long before skinhead gangs began appearing on the streets of cities all over America.

Skinheads can usually be recognized by their shaved or closely cropped heads and by the swastikas and other Nazi symbols they like to wear. Another standard part of the skinhead uniform is a pair of steel-toed Doc Marten boots. The boots are not just for show. They are weapons, used for kicking people. They are favored by some skinheads because they allow them to inflict as much damage as they could with brass knuckles or a steel pipe but with less risk of getting splashed with blood. Many skinheads seem afraid of blood. They worry about AIDS.

According to an ex-W.A.R. recruiter named Dave Mazzella, a high proportion of skinheads are dropouts. But some skinhead groups recruit on high school campuses. The Anti-Defamation League of B'nai B'rith has even reported one example of skinheads trying to recruit young members through their parents. The Confederate Hammer Skinheads sent flyers to parents of high school students in Waco, Texas, inviting parents to write for information on what skinheads were "doing to help the White schoolchildren in America."[10]

Skinheads pride themselves on their belligerent image, and some of them back up the image with violent action. According to the National Council of Churches, skinheads accounted for 121 known murders, 302 assaults, and 301 cross burnings in the mid-1980s alone.[11] Many of these crimes were directed against minorities.

Racist skinheads tend to identify racism as a central element of the belligerence that makes them a skinhead. "What makes a skinhead?" asked a Detroit skinhead. "Attitude. White Power. 'Cause niggers suck. Niggers and Jews. They're half monkeys, they should all be killed."[12]

Yet not all skinheads are white supremacists. Not all are even white. There are black, Hispanic, Native American, and even Asian skinheads as well. One black skinhead claimed that as far as he was concerned, there was no such thing as a racist skinhead. "We call them boneheads," he said.[13] Even some white skinheads look down on the racists as "loonies who give the rest of us a bad name."[14]

There have been violent clashes between nonracist skinhead gangs and "white power skins." In 1988, a nonracist gang called the Baldies drove the racist White Knights skinheads out of Minneapolis. The next year, nonracist skinheads from several states met in Minneapolis to form an umbrella group called the Syndicate.[15]

Still, the majority of America's skinheads are probably racists. There's no way to tell exactly how many of them there are. A December 1989 report issued by Klanwatch listed seventy different skinhead groups in the United States, some with chapters in six or seven different cities.[16] By far the largest skinhead group is Metzger's W.A.R. Skins, which may have as many as 1,400 members.[17] Altogether the Anti-Defamation League was already estimating the number of racist skinheads at around 3,000 by late 1989.[18] And the total seems to be growing.

White supremacists like the Metzgers hope that the skinheads will be their frontline troops in the race war they expect to come. To accomplish that, John Metzger has traveled around the country forging links between AYM/WSU and local skinhead groups. Skinhead leaders like Robert Heick of the American Front (San Francisco) and Michael Palesch of the National White Resistance (Metraire, Louisiana) have appeared together on national TV shows.

Outside observers doubt that Metzger will be able to unite all the skinheads into a single national organization. They are too independent, belligerent, and combative for that. But it hardly matters. Whether formally allied with AYM or not, the white power skinheads are already a vital part of the hate movement—maybe its single most violent part.

COMBING THE PRISONS

Many of the U.S. prisons are torn by conflict between white inmates and their black and Hispanic fellow prisoners. Some

Recruiter-in-chief for the white supremacy movement—Tom Metzger, found-er of the White Aryan Resistance (W.A.R.) and part-time television per-sonality. AP/WIDE WORLD

white supremacists have taken advantage of this fact to turn the prisons into recruiting grounds for the hate movement.

The most successful prison recruiting efforts seem to be those of Richard Butler and Robert Miles. Butler's Aryan Nations produces a newsletter, entitled *The Way,* specifically designed to appeal to white prisoners. Butler describes the white convicts as "prisoners of war," held by ZOG, the "Zionist Occupied Government" of the United States. According to the Anti-Defamation League, Butler's Aryan Nations has also been connected to an illegal gang known as the Aryan Brotherhood, operating inside prisons in at least two states.[19]

Robert Miles was once the Imperial Kludd (or chaplain) of the United Klans of America. For the past twenty years, he has run the Mountain Kirk (the Scottish term for "Church") in

Cohoctah, Michigan.[20] Although Miles preaches a theology of his own, which he calls "dualism," he is an old ally of Butler and other Identity types. He began what he calls his "Racial Theological Mission" to prisoners around the time he became one himself. That was in 1971, when he was convicted of blowing up some empty school buses used to integrate schools in Pontiac, Michigan. After his release, he intensified his "ministry." He recently claimed to be corresponding with 1,800 prisoners.[21]

Butler and Miles both maintain that their "ministries" are at least partly religious, but they have a clear political purpose as well: to persuade today's prisoners to enlist in the hate movement when they get out. Trained and hardened criminals, embittered by their prison experiences and committed to the cause of racism, they would make promising soldiers in the battle against blacks, Jews, and ZOG.

Miles sees the prisoners as the base of a powerful resurgence of white supremacy in the country at large. "The new political force may all be ex-cons!" he declares. "Almost 6,240,000 citizens of this land . . . [have been] convicted of state or federal felonies at one time or another in their lifetimes. How does that grab you as a political lobbying group?"[22]

It's a truly frightening thought.

9

Why People Join Hate Groups

Who belongs to hate groups, anyway? What kinds of people
are they? Not all of them shave their heads or wear swastika
tattoos. Most look and dress very much like other people. And,
for the most part, they live like other people, too. They raise
their families. They go to work. They go to school. They go to
movies and to sports events. Many consider themselves religious. On the outside, at least, they seem very much like
everyone else.

So, what makes them different? Why do they hate so much?
Why do they join organizations fundamentally opposed to the
ideals of equality and brotherhood which both their country
and their religions uphold?

There is no one answer to those questions. Many factors play
parts in making hate groups attractive to different people.
Some of those factors are social; that is, they have to do with
movements in society at large. Others are personal. They
involve the mental, emotional, and moral characters of the
people themselves.

SOCIAL UPHEAVAL

Hate groups grow best in times of social change. They get
many of their members from among those who feel most
threatened by the changes. The Ku Klux Klan, for instance,

was born in the turmoil of reconstruction. It found its recruits among the white southerners who feared losing their privileged place in society to the freed slaves. The second Klan found its members among those rural Americans who were frightened by the enormous social changes taking place after World War I. And the modern Klan was born out of the social disruption that resulted from the civil rights movement of the 1950s and 1960s.

A different kind of drastic social change helped set off a new wave of racism in the 1980s and early 1990s. This time, the upheaval was economic. Although many Americans prospered during this time, many poorer Americans did not. What's more, thousands of middle-class families saw their incomes plunge. Many families fell out of the middle class altogether. Some dropped all the way into poverty.

The children of these families provided many of the best recruits for the hate movement. As Leonard Zeskind, research director for the Center for Democratic Renewal, explains, "This is the first generation of white kids who don't expect to live better than their parents."[1] For some of them, the future seemed to be a terrifying place. Like the white southerners of an earlier time, they clung desperately to any group that promised to stop the changes—to hold back the future or, better still, restore an imaginary past.

That's what the hate groups do. They tell people that the nation is being taken over by African-Americans, Jews, Hispanic-Americans, Asian-Americans, and various foreigners. Join us, they say, and we will "take back" the country. Everything will be all right again. We will build a renewed, all-white America in which people like you will be in charge. America will return to an imagined past, when all that was necessary to be happy, secure, and prosperous was to be white.

Many young Americans don't realize that that past never existed. As Janet Caldwell of the Center for Democratic Renewal has said, "Young people are out of touch with [American] history."[2] They are unaware that America has been a multicultural society from the beginning. They know little about the long struggle for religious, racial, and political equality that has made the United States what it is.

They don't understand the social conditions they see around them, because they don't understand the past that created them. This tragic ignorance makes them ready to believe the distortions of history fed them by the likes of Richard Butler and the Metzgers. As Leonard Zeskind explains: "These kids have come to social consciousness in the age of Reagan, when affirmative action is a bad word and race relations are going backwards. They're alienated and fed up, and no one has reached them except for the right-wing crazies."[3]

IDEALISM

For some young people, the ideas of the right-wing crazies can seem like a true inspiration. Some even become involved in the hate movement out of a twisted sense of idealism, a desire to accomplish something worthwhile, to make the world a better place. In the 1950s and 1960s, for example, many people came to the hate movement through involvement in extreme anti-Communist political organizations like the John Birch Society. In those days, many idealistic Americans were angered by the way the Soviet Union had crushed the freedom of Eastern Europe. They feared that the Communist governments of the USSR and China would unite to conquer the United States and take over the world. Some of these people were drawn to the Klan and the Nazis because they seemed to be the only groups as opposed to Communism as they were. It is significant that the two leading "martyrs" of the hate movement—Bob Mathews of the Order, and Gordon Kahl of the Posse Comitatus—had both belonged to the John Birch Society. So had Tom Metzger.

Not everyone in the hate movement comes to it from the political right. The original members of the La Rouche group (see Chapter 10) came from the left-wing anti-Vietnam War movement in the 1960s. Others are moved by religious zeal. They believe that by joining the Klan or the Aryan Nations, they are fighting for Christianity or defending America against what an Identity spokesman has called "moral rot." For still others, race seems to take the place of religion. As Tom Metzger told the audience of the "Phil Donahue Show": "Our religion is of the race. Our highest religion is support of the race. . . . Everything else is secondary."[4]

THE NEED TO BELONG

Relatively few people join the hate movement out of idealism, however. Most join for personal reasons. One of the main motives that brings people to these groups is the need to belong. According to Morris Dees, an anti-white-supremacy lawyer who has had many clashes with hate group figures in court, many are "looking for something to join." They long for the chance "to be a part of something."[5]

Hate groups feed on people who are desperate and lonely. They like to reach them at times when they are particularly vulnerable. Dave Mazzella, who was once the best recruiter in Metzger's W.A.R. organization, explains that "groups like the Klan and W.A.R. . . . take advantage of people that are having problems in their life. They get people who are alienated, and they take advantage of them and they screw up their heads." Mazzella says that during his days with W.A.R., he would say anything he thought might attract a new member to the group. "I was a salesman," he explains. "I was a really good con man."[6]

Surprisingly, it's not just raging racists who join hate groups. Even Mazzella himself, who has left the hate movement and regrets ever being a part of it, denies that he was ever a racist. In fact, he says, hate group recruiters often downplay racism when they talk to potential members. At first, Mazzella explains, they simply try to present themselves as friends. "They talk about helping [potential recruits] out," he says. "The racism comes in later." Even then, "they rationalize everything. They make it sound like it's acceptable."[7] Eventually, many recruits simply accept racism as a necessary condition for belonging to the group.

AMBITION

Some people join hate groups out of simple ambition. They see the hate movement as a means of achieving personal glory, power, or profit—or all three at once. The most glaring early example of this was William J. Simmons, but he has had many imitators. For some hate group leaders, the hate movement is first and foremost a business. As attorney Morris Dees once said, referring to Tom Metzger, they are in the "unusual

"The skinheads are a family," says Joshua, a sixteen-year-old Nazi recruiter in Gilroy, California. "A lot of us don't have what you'd call a family unit at home. A lot of us don't have what you'd call a home." LONNY SHAVELSON/IMPACT VISUALS

business" of "making money out of selling hate."[8] It may be unusual, but it can be extremely profitable. Time and again, investigations have revealed that hate group leaders have enriched themselves at their followers' expense. A famous con man once said "there's a sucker born every minute," and the people who fall for hate group propaganda seem to be among them.

Some people who have no desire for economic profit look to the hate movement as an opportunity to make something of themselves—to be important. Many are people who have failed at everything else they've tried to do. They are, as Jane Nelson, whose husband was convicted of planning a hate group bombing, described the people she met in the Aryan Nations, "losers."[9] For such people, a hate group may be the only way they can imagine to do something with their lives, even if that something is violent, destructive, and ultimately pointless.

THE "POWER THING"

Some people are drawn to hate groups by a desire for excitement. They are attracted by what Bob Jones, a weapons expert who taught the White Patriot party to use explosives, described to a "Donahue" television audience as the "power thing."[10] In that sense, they are like little boys who have never grown up. They still dream of being Robin Hood, or Rambo, or the fastest gun in the West. They long for the sense of power that comes with being strong, and tough, and carrying a weapon.

Others have described this attraction as the warrior fantasy. Many people are attracted by it, but most of us realize that it is only a fantasy. Yet some hate group members imagine that they can live in that fantasy and make it real.

The warrior fantasy/hate group connection began when the founders of the Ku Klux Klan first decided to call themselves "knights." In much the same way, today's hate groups tend to surround themselves with the titles, the symbols, and the other trappings of war. Members of the Aryan Nations like to refer to themselves as "warriors," and leaders like the Metzgers flatter the skinheads by calling them the "shock troops" or "storm troopers" of the "white revolution."

It is no coincidence that many hate groups wear uniforms.

Klan members wear robes and hoods that suggest the helmets and robes medieval knights wore over their armor. Neo-Nazis like to strut around in military-style uniforms, complete with leather belts and boots. The survivalists of the Aryan Nations and similar groups outfit themselves with camouflage gear from military surplus stores. Paramilitary training camps, swastika tattoos, arm bands, Nazi-style salutes, flags, and even the Marine-recruit baldness of the skinheads all contribute to the warrior illusion. But the most obvious element of the entire fantasy of power is the hate movement's fascination with weapons. Like children playing with toys, Klan members, Nazis, and Aryan Nations members alike love to carry weapons of all kinds, from knives and hunting bows to semiautomatic rifles.

SELF-HATRED

Many of the people drawn to hate groups are emotionally deprived. Others are seriously disturbed. Published accounts of their lives often reveal unusually troubled childhoods. Typically, they grew up feeling a lot of anger, much of it directed at themselves. Psychologists believe that such childhoods often lead to feelings of terrible insecurity, even after the child has grown up.

Desperate to find an outlet for their anger, they look for someone to blame for their misery. That is why they latch onto the enemies presented to them by the hate movement. If they are failures in their lives, it must be because the Jews are conspiring against them. If they can't get a job, it must be because blacks are being unfairly favored. *I'm not to blame*, they tell themselves. *It's all their fault.*

Such people dream of being different than they are. Being weak, they dream of being strong. Being insecure, they dream of being in control. They long to impose their will on their surroundings and to make other people do what they want them to do.

Gordon Allport, a scholar who has studied the way prejudice develops in individuals, believes that insecurity is the real root of bigotry. The bigot—the kind of person most likely to join a hate group—is emotionally crippled. He (or she) "seems fearful of his own instinct, of his own consciousness, of change, of his

social environment. Since he cannot live in comfort with himself, or with others, he is forced to organize his whole style of
living, including his social attitudes, to fit his crippled condition." Such people, Allport explains, need a sense of order.
"Wherever possible, they latch onto what is familiar, safe,
simple, definite."[11]

People like that find safety and comfort in hate groups. The
hate movement gives them beliefs and activities to organize
their lives around. It tells them what to think and feel. It frees
them from the need to rely on their own insecure instincts and
feelings. At the same time, it gives them a false sense of power.
It gives them weapons and tells them they belong to an elite
race that has the right to rule the world.

As individuals, many of these people feel inferior and deeply
unworthy. The only way they know to feel valuable is to
believe that they belong to a valuable race. They *need* to feel
that their race is special in order to feel that they are special
themselves. Somehow, they hope, hating blacks, Jews, Catholics, and other minorities will make them feel better about
themselves. Whatever their personal faults and failures, they
tell themselves, at least they are *white*.

In many of these people, personal insecurity has festered
until it has turned into a deep self-hatred. An ex-member of
the Aryan Nations named David Cevette described this process
to a journalist named Doug Clark. "Aryan Nations members,"
he explained, "are so filled with such hatred that they [even
hate] themselves. Racism stems from nothing more than self-
hatred." Cevette admitted that he once felt the same way
himself. But he was wise enough to leave the hate movement
when he finally recognized his own feelings for what they were.
"I realized that I had no right to hate myself and then begin to
hate other people," he explained.[12] Sadly, many hate group
members never come to that realization.

10

Wolves in Sheep's Clothing

Most hate groups make no attempt to hide their racism. They glory in their support of white supremacy. They advertise it, parading around in white sheets, or wearing swastika badges, or lifting their arms in a Nazi salute. They openly call for violence against minorities and sometimes openly carry it out.

Not all the haters are that obvious—or that honest. Some are wolves in sheep's clothing. They hide their hatred behind a mask of reasonableness and respectability, pretending to be in the mainstream of American political life. They dress in business suits to look like ordinary politicians and use code words to sound like them. Instead of talking about "niggers," they talk about "welfare bums" and "undesirable elements." Instead of talking about "Jewish bankers" and "children of Satan," they talk about "Zionists" and "Israeli supporters."

By disguising their real beliefs and intentions, they trick unsophisticated people into supporting them. Masquerading as ordinary candidates, they steal the votes of many who would never dream of supporting the kind of hatred and bigotry they really represent.

WORKING WITHIN THE MAJOR POLITICAL PARTIES

White supremacists have long tried to find a place for themselves in the mainstream of American politics. At one time or another, they have tried to work their way inside each of the two major political parties. The Ku Klux Klan, for example, was extremely active in the 1920s, not only in national Democratic party politics, but in both Democratic and Republican party politics on the state level. It again became an important political force in the South in the days of the civil rights movement.

In the 1950s and 1960s, some of the haters found a foothold in the conservative right wing of the Republican party. They shared with most conservative Republicans a fierce opposition to Communism and a deep distrust of liberal government. On the surface it was sometimes hard to tell the difference between the beliefs of the most extreme right-wing Republicans and the most moderate members of the hate movements. People from both groups often met and mingled in the John Birch Society.

THE JOHN BIRCH SOCIETY

The John Birch Society was founded in 1958 in Indianapolis, Indiana. It was named after a young Baptist missionary to China who was killed by the Chinese Communists during World War II. The Society was not itself a hate group. It was not white supremacist and did not call for violence against minorities. But in the early 1960s it shared many beliefs with both the most conservative elements of the Republican and Democratic parties on the one hand, and the neo-Nazi and Identity groups on the other.

Like them, it was fanatically anti-Communist. Like them, it opposed the income tax and considered the social security system a giant step on the road toward Socialism. And Socialism, they believed, was only a baby step away from the great evil of Communism itself.

Like many hate groups, the Birch Society was marked by a kind of paranoia—a deep distrust and suspicion toward everyone who didn't share its views. It saw Communism as a vast international conspiracy and suspected almost every imaginable institution of being a part of that conspiracy. The most extreme of the Birchers were convinced that U.S. government itself was a tool of the Communists. The Society's founder,

Robert Welch, once charged even the Republican president, Dwight D. Eisenhower, with being a tool of the Communist conspiracy.

Such statements led some observers to dismiss the Birch Society. They considered it so far out on the "lunatic fringe" of American politics that it couldn't be taken seriously. As it turned out, however, the John Birch Society had a significant impact on the politics of the early 1960s.

The Society was particularly effective at reaching young people. Perhaps this was because the young have little experience with the real world of international politics and little knowledge of recent history. In any case, many young Americans were persuaded by the Birchers' theory that a massive conspiracy was threatening the world, and that the U.S. government was already half in the enemy camp. Those who believed this theory became easy prey for the racist theories of the hate groups who claimed that the Jews were in league with the Communists in the great conspiracy. Among the young people influenced by the writings of Robert Welch was Robert Mathews, who later founded the Order.[1]

The Birch Society was a significant force in the Republican party in some conservative states, including Arizona, where Birchers played a key role in conservative Senator Barry Goldwater's campaign for president in 1964. Bircher delegates helped Goldwater win the nomination at the Republican national convention that year, although he lost the actual election in a landslide to the Democratic president, Lyndon Johnson.[2]

Goldwater was not personally a member of the Birch Society, although he accepted their support. Nor was Goldwater a hater. But a man who was both was making inroads in the Republican party in California around the same time. That man was William Potter Gale, the guiding spirit of the Identity movement. In the same year that Goldwater ran for president, Gale ran in the Republican primary for governor of California. Four years later, he tried for the Republican nomination for Congress. He lost both times. Most of the other open bigots who have tried to win nominations from either of the two major parties have lost as well. But that doesn't mean they've stopped trying.

LYNDON LA ROUCHE

At least one hate group figure tried to enter the mainstream of national politics from the top, as a presidential candidate. He was Lyndon La Rouche, the founder of organizations with names like the National Caucus of Labor Committees (NCLC) and the National Democratic Policy Committee. Despite their names, the La Rouche groups were not associated with either organized labor or the Democratic party. Instead, they were tools of a political cult centered on La Rouche and his peculiar view of the world.

La Rouche is one of the few hate movement figures who began on the political left instead of the political right. During the 1960s, he led a spinoff of a leftist student organization known as the Students for a Democratic Society, or SDS. La Rouche called his group the SDS Labor Committee until he changed its name to the National Caucus of Labor Committees.[3]

By the late 1970s, it was clear that the La Rouche movement had less in common with the leftist SDS than with the neo-Nazis. For one thing, the NCLC was totally centered on La Rouche himself, much the way the German Nazi party had been centered on Hitler. For another, La Rouche's view of the world was based on a version of the old Jewish-conspiracy theory.

La Rouche's version has some peculiar wrinkles, however. He insists that the center of the conspiracy is in Great Britain, which he claims is secretly controlled by Jewish bankers, led by the Rothschild family. In La Rouche's view, the queen of England, the Rockefeller family of the United States, the government of Israel, many leaders of the Soviet Union, and hordes of secret "Zionists" around the world are all involved with the Rothschilds in this enormous conspiracy. Its ultimate aim is nothing less than the total destruction of the human race.

In order to defeat this conspiracy, La Rouche apparently wants to establish a dictatorship in the United States, presumably with himself as dictator. The dictator would stamp out the conspirators wherever they were found. Although he doesn't spell it out, this sounds much like a modern pogrom against the

Jews. And, unless the Soviet Union was ready to do the same to its own secret Zionists, a "total war" against the Soviets might be needed as well.

La Rouche attempted to gain national attention by running for president several times in the 1970s and 1980s. Sometimes he ran as an independent and sometimes as a candidate in Democratic party primaries. In 1984, he managed to get himself on the ballot, as an independent, in seventeen states. La Rouche never won a significant number of votes in any of the elections and never won a single electoral vote. Still, he made himself nationally known by buying large chunks of television campaign time, which he used to present the so-called British conspiracy theory to the American public.

In his TV spots, La Rouche looked like a prosperous businessman and sounded like a mild-mannered college professor. He spoke quietly and reasonably, as though he were lecturing a first-year class. He said nothing jarringly racist. And, in fact, he was so careful about what he said that it was difficult for most viewers to understand what he was driving at. The ads were professionally produced, and many unsuspecting viewers must have thought they were watching a legitimate Democratic party candidate. To some of them, at least, the well-spoken La Rouche must have seemed like an attractive candidate. Some of them were undoubtedly inspired to contribute to his campaign, and some must have found themselves drawn into the web of anti-Semitic nonsense that La Rouche was weaving.

Just as La Rouche ran for president, his followers sometimes ran for state and local office as well. Like La Rouche himself, they sometimes ran as Democrats, sometimes as independents, and sometimes even as Republicans. The party label didn't matter to them. Their purpose was to get elected, and then to use their office to promote La Rouche's cause. In places where the local Democratic and Republican parties didn't realize what was going on quickly enough, some La Rouchies actually won a major party's nomination.

The La Rouchies' tactics got national attention when one of their candidates won the Democratic nomination for secretary of state of Illinois. Their scatter-gun approach—operating as independents at the same time within both major parties—has been called the "tri-partisan strategy." Other elements of the hate movement seem to be taking it up.

The La Rouche movement has been essentially a one-man show, a cult built around the personality and ideas of Lyndon La Rouche. Like many other cult leaders, La Rouche demanded two things from his followers: absolute personal loyalty to their leader, and financial support. According to people who left the cult, some members actually tithed—gave a tenth of all their income—to the cult. A few even turned over their entire life's savings to the movement.[4]

Late in the 1980s, La Rouche and several of his lieutenants were charged with fraud in the way they raised and managed funds. Their convictions have badly damaged the La Rouche movement. It remains to be seen if it has been destroyed.

THE POPULIST PARTY

In 1984, a group of neo-Nazis, Klan and Posse Comitatus leaders, and far-right activists of other kinds joined together to form the Populist party. They hoped to use it to establish a national political base for themselves. Within a year, they had laid the foundation of a political organization in forty-nine states.[5] Despite its national ambitions, however, the party's main strength continued to be in the West and the midwestern farm belt.

The Populist—or "People's"—party took its name from a party that had tried to unite American farmers and workers to oppose the growing power of big business in the late nineteenth century. Although the party lasted only a few years, it represented the views of many thousands of rural Americans. In 1892, its presidential candidate won over a million popular votes and twenty-two electoral votes. The party died out only because the larger Democratic party adopted most of its policies.

The new Populist party is nowhere near as large as the old. In fact, it has little in common with its nineteenth-century namesake except its name. The first Populists thought of "the people" and the federal government as being the same thing. Their party platform called for giving the government greater powers "to the end that oppression, injustice, and poverty shall eventually cease in the land."[6] The new Populists, on the other hand, regard the government as an enemy.

The original Populists campaigned in favor of a federal income tax. They saw it as a way to spread the nation's wealth more evenly. The new Populists hate the income tax and resent having to share their wealth with those poorer than themselves. The first Populists opposed using gold and silver as money. They wanted the government to print paper money, so there would be plenty of money available to people when times were hard. The new Populists want to end the authority of the U.S. Federal Reserve Board to do just that.

The new Populist party is little more than a hate group in disguise. Its first chairman was a onetime Grand Dragon of the Mississippi Klan named Robert Weems, but the real power behind the scenes seems to have been Willis Carto. Carto is known as one of the country's leading propagandists for hate. He runs both the so-called Liberty Lobby, the nation's most active anti-Semitic propaganda mill, and Noontide Press, a major publisher of neo-Nazi literature. He also publishes the most widely read anti-Semitic newspaper in the country, *The Spotlight*.[7] From the start, Carto used his paper—a thirty-two-page weekly, with 115,000 subscribers around the country—to champion the Populist party.

Despite the party's many connections to known racists (like Carto, the Klan, the Posse, and the neo-Nazi National States Rights party) it tries to maintain an image of responsibility. For a time, its disguise seemed to be successful. It scored a propaganda coup when it convinced a popular ex-Olympic champion pole vaulter named Bob Richards to be its first candidate for president of the United States. Richards pulled out, however, when he realized that running as a Populist would brand him as a front for die-hard racists.

Not long after it was founded, the Populist party was split by a power struggle between Carto and other party leaders. In the process, it lost most of its organization and popular support in the Midwest. Carto took total control of what was left. Today, most of the party's strength seems to be confined to Pennsylvania and a few of the western states. Even so, the Populists still hope to be seen as a responsible third party: a real

alternative for those frustrated Americans who find themselves
to the right of the two major political parties. Despite its
attempts to hide its real nature, however, it remains, in the
words of the conservative political commentator George Will,
"a salad of extremists."[8]

DAVID DUKE

So far in the early 1990s, the most successful of all the wolves
in sheep's clothing has been an ex-Klan leader named David
Duke. Despite his ties to the Klan and other branches of the
hate movement, he still managed to win election to the Louisiana legislature in 1988 and again in 1990. What's more, after
losing an election for Louisiana governor in 1991, he declared
his candidacy for the Republican nomination for president in
1992.

Now in his early forties, Duke first got involved in the politics
of bigotry as a teenager, and he has been involved with it ever
since. He joined the Ku Klux Klan while he was still in high
school and founded a neo-Nazi-style organization he called the
White Youth Alliance while he was a student at Louisiana State
University. While there, he attended at least one demonstra-
tion wearing a Nazi-style uniform. In 1975, he became a major
figure in white supremacy circles as head of the Knights of the
Ku Klux Klan, or KKKK for short.

Five years later, he was publicly embarrassed when he was
caught trying to sell the KKKK membership list to another
Klan leader, Bill Wilkinson.[9] Resigning from the KKKK, he
soon founded a new organization called the National Association for the Advancement of White People, or NAAWP. The
name is a takeoff (or send up) of the National Association for
the Advancement of Colored People, the organization which
has fought for civil rights for black Americans since 1910. The
NAAWP claims that it is a public interest group, working to
protect the rights of white people. But, in the words of Reverend James C. Carter, president of Loyola University, Duke's
NAAWP "is little more than the continued advocacy of the
anti-black, anti-Catholic, and anti-Semitic policies of the
[K]lan."[10]

Like Lyndon La Rouche, Duke has followed a strategy of
running as a candidate for any party that will have him. Unlike

La Rouche, he has been successful at it. This came as no surprise to the antiracist Center for Democratic Renewal, which predicted early on that Duke's "down home racism" would prove more successful than La Rouche's "conspiracy theories."[11]

In recent years, Duke has tried to improve his image in more ways than one. Physically, he has apparently had four plastic surgery operations to improve his looks. Politically, he has tried to distance himself from his past. He now claims that his Klan and Nazi activities were nothing more than "pranks" and "youthful mistakes." Like many southerners in the 1960s, he explains, he joined the Klan in reaction to the civil rights movement. "I joined," he told Phil Donahue's TV audience, "because I came to believe that white people in America were losing their basic rights. . . . [T]he only group I saw standing up was the Klan, and [in] my particular community it was a legal, law abiding organization." As for his past association with Nazism, he now claims to "condemn . . . any sort of totalitarianism, whether it be fascism, or Nazism, or communism."[12]

Duke does not specifically admit that he is a racist, although he has admitted that he believes in "race science." Instead, he uses political "code words" that make his real beliefs clear to his supporters, without ever spelling them out. When he condemns "crime" and "criminals," for example, his supporters understand that he is talking about blacks. After all, he says, black people "have more of a tendency to act in anti-social ways" than white people do.[13] When he talks about the "massive illegitimate birth rate among welfare recipients," he is really talking about single black women having children. When he talks about ensuring "equal rights for all Americans," he is really talking about taking away the rights of black Americans.[14]

In his speeches, he calls for an end to virtually every measure adopted to help black people overcome the effects of the generations of racial discrimination they've suffered. He particularly detests the affirmative action programs that enlarge the opportunities for black people in the education system and job markets. In addition, he calls for major changes in the welfare system, including new measures to discourage, if not actually

The most successful of all the wolves in sheep's clothing—David Duke.
COPYRIGHT, SHIA PHOTO, 1990/IMPACT VISUALS

prevent, poor black women from having children. He has also suggested measures to encourage people with high IQs—most of whom he seems to assume would be white—to have children.[15]

As a politician, Duke continues to seek, and win, the support of known racists. In 1988, for example, he accepted the Populist party nomination for president. One of his first public appearances after his election to the Louisiana House was at a Populist meeting in Chicago. While there, he was photographed shaking hands with a prominent American Nazi party official. Duke later claimed he didn't know who the man was. Maybe he didn't, but around the same time Duke was selling Nazi literature out of his own office back in Louisiana. What's more, his office telephone number was apparently the same as that of the local Klan organization!

Among those who were not fooled by Duke's political makeover was the late Lee Atwater, who at the time was chairman of the Republican National Committee. Shortly after Duke was elected to the Louisiana House as a Republican, Atwater made clear that the national Republican party wanted nothing to do with Duke. "He's a pretender," Atwater publicly declared, "a charlatan and a political opportunist who is looking for any organization he can find to legitimize his views of racial and religious bigotry."[16] So far, however, the Louisiana Republican party has not repudiated him as well.

In 1990, Duke ran in the Louisiana primary as a Republican candidate for the U.S. Senate. It was an open primary, in which both Republicans and Democrats could run. If a candidate for either party got over half of all the votes cast, he or she would be elected. Duke and another Republican, Ben Bagert, were the leading Republicans. The Democrats pinned their chances on the incumbent senator, J. Bennett Johnston.

Everyone knew who David Duke was and what his connections were. Eight Republican senators actually endorsed the Democratic candidate in order to discourage their fellow Republicans from voting for a well-known bigot. Finally, even Duke's Republican opponent, Ben Bagert, pulled out of the election in hopes of throwing his voters to the Democrat.

The Democrat Johnston won more than 50 percent of the

total vote and kept his Senate seat. But, in losing, David Duke got 44 percent of the total vote, nearly double what the polls had predicted. What's more, Duke's 44 percent included 56 percent of the votes cast by all the white voters in the statewide election!

It wasn't clear how many Duke voters voted for him *because* of his associations with white supremacy and how many voted for him *in spite of* them. But the result shocked political observers around the country. Duke's showing didn't necessarily mean that most white voters in Louisiana wanted to return to segregation. It didn't even mean that they were racist. But it did mean that they didn't mind voting for someone who was.

As Lance Hill, head of the anti-Duke Louisiana Coalition, put it, "There's little doubt that the majority of white people in this state are willing to put a man in power who spent his whole life agitating hatred against blacks and Jews."[17] People like Hill were disheartened by this fact, but white supremacists were delighted. For the first time since the end of the civil rights movement of the 1960s, it seemed that racism was becoming politically respectable again—at least in Louisiana.

11

Fighting Hate

It is important not to underestimate the hate movement, but it is important not to overestimate the hate movement either. There have been times—in the 1920s, for instance—when a group like the Ku Klux Klan actually represented a large segment of American society. But not anymore. Even by the most generous estimates, hate group members and sympathizers add up to only a tiny fraction of the American population. What's more, it is not even a very influential fraction. For the most part, these are not people whom other people listen to, much less follow. Few hold positions of real respect, authority, or power. The hate groups exist on the outer fringes of American society, not at its center.

How Strong Is the Hate Movement Today?

That is a difficult question to answer. Hate groups come and go. It is hard even to tell how many groups are active at any given moment, much less how many members they have. Hate groups keep their membership lists secret for a variety of reasons. Some brag about how many members they have, but their claims are probably inflated, since they know there's no way to prove them wrong. And, even if the groups gave out the real numbers, the raw figures would still be misleading.

For one thing, the hate movement includes many people who

never bother to join an organized group. Observers estimate that for every hate group member, there are probably seven to ten more or less active sympathizers. All the Ku Klux Klan groups combined probably have no more than 4,500 to 5,500 members,[1] for example, but there may be as many as 55,000 Klan sympathizers altogether. What's more, there are probably thousands more who are influenced to some extent by Klan propaganda. Much the same could be said for all the Nazi, Identity, skinhead, and other hate groups as well. On the other hand, there is a lot of cross-membership between hate groups. People dedicated to the hate movement often belong to several groups at the same time, swelling the membership lists of all of them.

Even knowing how many groups there are doesn't tell you much about their strength. In 1989, the Klanwatch Project of the Southern Poverty Law Center counted 205 white suprem-

Could this be the future? CATHERINE SMITH/IMPACT VISUALS

acist groups in the United States. They included fifty-three Klan groups, twenty-six neo-Nazi groups, thirty-eight Christian Identity groups, six Posse Comitatus groups, seventy Skinhead groups, and twelve other hate organizations.[2] But these groups vary drastically in size, as well as in activities. The biggest of them (like KKKK, and the W.A.R. Skins) claim to have more than 1,000 members each; the smallest consist of nothing more than a few fanatics with an impressive-sounding name and a mailing address.

Even the number of groups within a particular branch of the hate movement says little. There are more neo-Nazi groups now than there were ten years ago, for instance, but that doesn't mean that the Nazis are stronger today than they used to be. In fact, it probably means just the opposite. The main reason there are more groups now is the fact that the larger groups have broken up into a collection of smaller and less powerful organizations.

Most observers believe that the overall hate movement reached a temporary peak in the early to mid-1980s. Since then, most of the movement has declined; only the skinheads have grown dramatically in size and strength.

Interviewed on the C-SPAN television network in 1990, Colonel Leonard Supenski, a hate crimes expert from the Baltimore County Police Department, put the numbers in perspective: "In terms of the organized hate groups . . . we're probably dealing with a small number when [compared to] the totality of the American population. Probably about 20,000 real dedicated activists in hate group activities, and about another 150,000 sympathizers." That's certainly a lot of haters, Colonel Supenski admits, but it's clearly "not representative of mainstream America."

Hate groups do represent a threat to American society. They work against America's most basic principles and moral values. What's more, they can be physically dangerous for members of minority groups, and for anyone else who opposes them. But, even after all that has been said, they are much less powerful than they sometimes appear to be. Time and again, it has been proven that these groups can be fought—and beaten.

Throwing Light on the Shadows

Ever since the night riders of the Ku Klux Klan first started visiting freed slaves' cabins under cover of darkness, hate groups have operated best in the darkness and shadows. They have organized in secret and struck in the dark. One of the best ways to fight them is simply to remove the shadows they move in, and the easiest way to get rid of a shadow is to throw light on it.

Hate groups find it hard to function out in the open, in the bright light of the day. When the truth about their beliefs and activities is known, it is harder for them to fool well-meaning people into accepting their arguments. Even more important, reports of their activities alert the general public to the danger these groups represent. They may even provoke disgust among some hate group members themselves, who haven't realized how far their comrades are going.

Again and again, experience has shown that truth is one of the most powerful weapons that can be used against the haters. Press exposure of the Klan's political ties helped to end its political power in the 1920s, while exposure of its financial corruption led to its total collapse. Forty years later, press and congressional reports of the Klan's violence once again helped to arouse opposition to it.

Law Enforcement

One of the things that most distinguishes hate groups is their encouraging of criminal acts of violence against minorities. It is important to find and prosecute the people who actually carry out these crimes, but it is just as important to establish the guilt of those who encouraged them to commit them.

For decades, law enforcement officials were slow to recognize the real nature of hate groups. They prosecuted the crimes that members committed on a case-by-case basis, the way they would prosecute any isolated mugging or murder. But they failed to acknowledge that it was the hate groups themselves that were often responsible for these crimes.

Sometime in the mid-1980s, federal law enforcement officials began to wake up to the danger the hate groups represent.

They decided to treat them the way they treat other organized crime organizations, such as Mafia families and drug rings. Besides charging individuals with specific violent actions, they began prosecuting hate movement leaders under federal racketeering laws that make it illegal to run what the law calls an "ongoing criminal enterprise."

Several states jumped in with prosecutions of their own. At least eighteen passed laws banning paramilitary training within their borders. This made the kind of terrorist training carried on by groups like the CSA illegal.

The result of all this, according to the Anti-Defamation League of B'nai B'rith, was "the most sweeping crackdown on the far-right in the United States since World War II."[3] This crackdown sent much of the hate movement reeling. Many movement leaders were prosecuted, and scores of them went to jail.

Abandoning what they had once claimed were their high principles, several turned informer and testified against their ex-comrades in the movement. The turncoats included some of the big names in the hate movement, including James Ellison of the CSA and Glenn Miller of the White Patriot party. Some testified in return for lighter sentences. Others—like skinhead Dave Mazzella and Order member Tom Martinez—acted in honest revulsion at what they had done while in the movement.

By the late 1980s, over fifty hate group leaders had been imprisoned. Although some of them received sentences of only a few weeks or months, others were given much longer terms. Many of these are still in prison and will be there for a long time to come. David Tate, an Order member who murdered a policeman for stopping him for a traffic violation in 1985, was sentenced to life imprisonment without parole. Bruce Pierce, a close companion of Robert Mathews, got a total of 252 years for a variety of crimes, ranging from counterfeiting to taking part in the killing of radio talk show host Alan Berg. Probably the best known among the jailed leaders was presidential candidate Lyndon La Rouche. In 1989, he was sentenced to fifteen years in prison for financial fraud in connection with the raising and spending of campaign funds.

Not all the efforts to convict hate group leaders have been

successful. In fact, the federal government failed in its most ambitious attempt to prosecute hate movement leaders. In February 1987, thirteen white supremacist leaders were indicted in Fort Smith, Arkansas. Nine of them were charged with conspiracy to overthrow the U.S. government. Five were charged with conspiracy to murder a judge. The case was special because it tied together so many important figures in a single prosecution. Among those indicted were Richard Butler; Louis Beam, an ex-KKKK official and Aryan Nations leader who had been captured while on the FBI's Ten-Most-Wanted List; and Robert Miles, the pastor of the Mountain Church, who was prominent in almost every branch of the movement, including the Klan, the Aryan Nations, and Christian Identity.

The Fort Smith prosecution was based largely on the testimony of informers, especially James Ellison, "King James of the Ozarks." Apparently, the jury found it hard to take their word and acquitted the defendants. Seven of the thirteen went free. The other six were returned to the various prisons where they were already serving sentences for other crimes. Nonetheless, the hate movement considered the mass acquittal a great victory. Outside the courthouse, a happy Louis Beam told the press that ZOG had suffered a "terrible blow."[4]

Despite this major setback, the federal government has continued its campaign against the haters. In addition to greater use of the antiracketeering laws, it has taken advantage of federal civil rights laws to prosecute people who use violence against members of minority groups. The government won 169 convictions under such laws between October 1987 and April 1989 alone, the last period for which figures are available.[5]

Hate criminals are being tried and convicted at a higher rate than ever before. This is not to say that all hate criminals are caught, much less convicted. In fact, most hate crimes, like most other violent crimes, still go unpunished. But enough of these hate criminals are being caught and imprisoned to put more pressure on the hate groups than ever before. The government has served notice that the encouragement of violence against minority groups is not tolerable in our society.

CIVIL SUITS

In 1979, a group of Klansmen and neo-Nazis attacked an anti-Klan "Death to the Klan" march in Greensboro, North Caro-

lina. Five anti-Klan demonstrators were killed. Criminal trials
following the murderous attack failed to convict the killers.
Although it seemed fairly clear who had been responsible,
there was apparently not enough evidence for a criminal conviction.

Not willing to leave it there, relatives of the murdered
demonstrators sued several Klansmen in civil court, where the
rules are different than they are in criminal court. And there,
they were able to win a verdict against them.[6] The financial
judgment was not as satisfying to the angry relatives as sending
the killers to jail would have been, but the suit demonstrated
another way of making the haters pay for their crimes.

In another case, in 1982, Klansmen in Tennessee were
ordered to pay $535,000 to five elderly black women injured
when the Klan shot up a black neighborhood in Chattanooga
two years before.

The civil suit may prove to be the most powerful weapon yet
found against hate groups. In fact, it has already been used to
destroy one of the largest and most powerful Klans in the
country, the United Klans of America. The case grew out of a
particularly brutal murder in Mobile, Alabama, in March
1981. Racial tensions were running high in Mobile at that time.
A black man had been on trial for the murder of a white
policeman, and the jury couldn't agree on a verdict. On the
night of March 21, there was a Klan meeting at the Mobile
home of Bennie Hays, a high-ranking UKA official. Klan
members were angry about the hung jury. As they saw it, a
black man was getting away with killing a white man. They
wanted revenge. A life for a life. Two Klansmen left Hays's
home that night looking for someone black to kill.

Prowling through the streets in a car, they found a nineteen-
year-old black man named Michael Donald walking alone.
They forced him into the car at gunpoint and drove him several
miles away to a deserted spot. There, they beat him viciously,
strangled him with a rope, and slit his throat. Then they drove
back to Mobile and hung his body from a tree limb.

Two years later, the killers were convicted of their crime.
But Michael's mother, Beulah Mae Donald, was not content to
leave it at that. She enlisted the aid of Morris Dees, a civil

rights crusader who'd helped found the Southern Poverty Law Center in Montgomery, Alabama, and an attorney and state senator named Michael A. Figures. With their help, she sued the killers—and most important, the United Klans of America as well. Her suit argued that the killers had not been acting on their own. They had, in fact, been carrying out the policy of the UKA to abuse and murder black people. Therefore, Mrs. Donald's lawyers argued, the UKA was responsible for what its "agents" had done.

At the trial, a remorseful young Klansman who had helped to kill Michael Donald agreed. He told the court, "I was acting as a Klansman when I done this. And I hope that people learn from my mistake. . . . I do hope you decide a judgment against me and everyone else involved."[7] The jury did just that. Within a few hours it announced a judgment of $7 million against the UKA.

The UKA didn't have anywhere near that amount of money, so in May 1987, it was forced to surrender to Mrs. Donald the only thing it did have that was worth much at all: the building that served as the UKA's national headquarters in Tuscaloosa, Alabama. The little building was eventually sold for about $55,000, a pitifully small amount of money in return for a young man's life. However, the suit won something more important than money. It bankrupted the United Klans of America, destroying what had been the second largest hate group in the entire country.

An even bigger judgment was handed down against Tom Metzger and W.A.R. in October 1990. Almost two years earlier, members of a skinhead group called the East Side White Pride had murdered Mulugeta Seraw, a twenty-eight-year-old black Ethiopian student, in Portland, Oregon. They had beaten him to death with a baseball bat, while their girlfriends watched from a nearby car, screaming encouragement.

Discovering that the Portland skinheads had been incited to commit violence by a recruiter from Metzger's organization, the Southern Poverty Law Center sued. A Portland jury passed down a whopping $12 million judgment against the Metzgers and W.A.R. Appearing before the TV cameras after the verdict, Tom Metzger insisted that the white supremacy movement would survive. "The white racist movement . . . will not be stopped in the puny town of Portland," Metzger proclaimed. "We're too deep. We're embedded now. Don't you understand? We're in your colleges, we're in your army, we're in your police forces."[8] But, as Morris Dees has pointed out, Tom Metzger is selling his house. The Metzgers and W.A.R. have been dealt a blow from which they are unlikely to recover.

TOWARD A VICTORY OVER HATE

The legal victories described above are impressive. They have contributed greatly to the decline in the size and power of the traditional hate groups in recent years. But damaging, and even destroying, particular groups is not enough to destroy the hate movement itself. "The white racist movement," as Tom Metzger proclaimed in Portland, is far from dead. Even its decline may be only temporary.

If the hate movement is going to be destroyed, it will take much more than aggressive law enforcement and civil lawsuits. The courts are an important battlefield in the war against hatred and violence, but the decisive battles will not be fought there. They will be fought in society at large.

The final defeat of the hate movement will require the combined efforts of many elements of society. In the words of a Klanwatch Intelligence Report: "It . . . demands the attention of every citizen. For legislators, it means refining laws to address the serious threat of hate crime. For educators, it means finding ways to open the channels of cultural understanding among children. For police, it means increased attention to acts of hate violence. For neighborhoods, it means strengthening the bonds of community to embrace diversity and reject acts of bigotry. And for every individual, it means seeking understanding in the place of resentment, and desiring peace in the place of conflict."[9] Most of all, it will require the efforts of all people of goodwill, whatever their color, background, or religion.

The hate movement thrives on social tensions. Like a poisonous plant that gets nourishment from toxic chemicals, it feeds on the hostility among racial, ethnic, and religious groups. The prejudice, ignorance, and distrust that produce this hostility are much more dangerous than the hate movement itself. To the extent that we can overcome these evils—through understanding, tolerance, and goodwill—the hate groups will lose the source of their hatred. Like poisonous plants robbed of nourishment, they will be left to wither and die.

Notes

1. The Heritage of Hate

1. Gary Gerhardt, "City Police Discount Former Klan Leader's Claim in Berg's Death," *Rocky Mountain News*, January 11, 1985; "Order Killers Targeted Jewish Talk Show Host," in *The Ku Klux Klan: A History of Racism and Violence* (Montgomery, Ala.: Klanwatch, 1988), p. 43; Kevin Flynn and Gary Gerhardt, *The Silent Brotherhood* (New York: Signet, 1990), pp. 249–50.

2. Fred R. Holmes, *Prejudice and Discrimination* (Englewood Cliffs, N.J.: Prentice Hall, 1970), p. 5.

2. "We Hold These Truths"

1. John F. Kennedy, *A Nation of Immigrants*, rev. ed. (New York: Harper and Row, 1964), pp. 2–3.

2. Ibid., p. 11.

3. J. Hector St. John Crèvecoeur, *Letters From an American Farmer*, in *Impressions of America*, selected and edited by Ralph A. Brown and Marian R. Brown (New York: Harcourt, Brace and World, 1966), pp. 55–57.

4. Michael Banton, *Race Relations* (New York: Basic Books, 1967), p. 12.

5. James McPherson, the author of the upcoming book, *Lincoln and the Second American Revolution*, interviewed over Wisconsin Public Radio in April 1991.

6. James Ford Rhodes, "Antecedents of the American Civil War," in *The Causes of the American Civil War*, edited by Edwin C. Rozwenc (Lexington, Mass.: Heath, 1972), p. 52.

7. The actual figures, as of 1860 when the Civil War started (3,950,513 slaves, 383,637 slaveowners, and roughly 8 million white southerners), come from *American History: A Survey,* by Richard N. Current, T. Harry Williams, and Frank Freidel, 4th ed. (New York: Knopf, 1975), p. 327.

8. Kennedy, *A Nation of Immigrants,* p. 91.

9. "The Civil War," a PBS television documentary series, Florentine Films, Ken Burns, writer/producer, 1989.

3. HATRED ON HORSEBACK

1. *The Ku Klux Klan: A History of Racism and Violence* (Montgomery, Ala.: Klanwatch, 1988), p. 49.

2. Ibid., p. 8.

3. Quoted in "1872: Visitor from Hell," in "Mark of the Beast," a special edition of *Southern Exposure,* Summer 1980, p. 14.

4. Richard N. Current, T. Harry Williams, and Frank Freidel, *American History: A Survey,* 4th ed. (New York: Knopf, 1975), p. 429.

5. *Funk and Wagnall's New Encyclopedia* (Funk and Wagnalls, 1986), vol. 15, p. 328.

6. *Hate Groups in America, A Record of Bigotry and Violence* (New York: Anti-Defamation League of B'nai B'rith, 1988), p. 75.

7. Ibid.

4. HATRED FOR FUN AND PROFIT

1. Wyn Craig Wade, *The Fiery Cross* (New York: Simon and Schuster, 1987), p. 13. This book, which is a history of the KKK, should not be confused with the Klan periodical of the same name.

2. *Hate Groups in America, A Record of Bigotry and Violence* (New York: Anti-Defamation League of B'nai B'rith, 1988), p. 76.

3. Fred J. Cook, *The Ku Klux Klan: America's Recurring Nightmare* (New York: Julian Messner, 1989), p. 37.

4. Wade, *The Fiery Cross,* p. 150.

5. Ibid.

6. Thomas F. Gossett, *Race: The History of an Idea in America* (Dallas: Southern Methodist University Press, 1963), p. 340.

7. Wade, *The Fiery Cross,* p. 155.

8. Ibid., p. 202.

9. *The Ku Klux Klan: A History of Racism and Violence* (Montgomery, Ala.: Klanwatch, 1988), p. 16.

10. Ibid., p. 18.

5. The Klan's Losing Battle to Save Jim Crow

1. Richard N. Current, T. Harry Williams, and Frank Freidel, *American History: A Survey,* 4th ed. (New York: Knopf, 1975), p. 782.

2. *Chronicle of the 20th Century* (Mount Kisco, N.Y.: Chronicle Publications, 1987), p. 753.

3. *Hate Groups in America, A Record of Bigotry and Violence* (New York: Anti-Defamation League of B'nai B'rith, 1988), pp. 80–86.

4. Ibid.

5. *Chronicle,* p. 942.

6. Talk given on June 9, 1979, quoted in "The Klan Speaks," in "Mark of the Beast," a special edition of *Southern Exposure,* Summer 1980, p. 40.

7. Wyn Craig Wade, *The Fiery Cross* (New York: Simon and Schuster, 1987), pp. 442–43.

8. "The Klan Speaks," p. 40.

9. Ibid.

10. *Hate Groups in America, A Record of Bigotry and Violence,* p. 8.

11. *The Ku Klux Klan: A History of Racism and Violence* (Montgomery, Ala.: Klanwatch, 1988), p. 51.

6. The Ghost of Adolf Hitler

1. In the Foreword to Michael Billig's *Psychology, Racism & Facism* (Birmingham, England: Searchlight, 1979).

2. *Hate Groups in America, A Record of Bigotry and Violence* (New York: Anti-Defamation League of B'nai B'rith, 1988), p. 24.

3. Gary E. McCuen, ed. *The Racist Reader* (Anoka, Minn.: Greenhaven Press, 1974), p. 123.

4. *Hate Groups in America, A Record of Bigotry and Violence,* p. 26.

5. Ibid., p. 27.

6. Andrew MacDonald, *The Turner Diaries* (Arlington, Va.: National Alliance, 1978).

7. *Hate Groups in America, A Record of Bigotry and Violence,* p. 27.

8. For more on the Minutemen, see J. Harvy Jones Jr., *The Minutemen* (Garden City, N.Y.: Doubleday, 1968).

9. Kevin Flynn and Gary Gerhardt, *The Silent Brotherhood* (New York: Signet, 1989), p. 420.

10. *Hate Groups in America, A Record of Bigotry and Violence,* p. 42.

11. Flynn and Gerhardt, *The Silent Brotherhood,* pp. 446–47.

12. Ibid., pp. 464–65.

7. A CASE OF MISTAKEN IDENTITY

1. From Wesley Swift, *Anti-Christ in the Pulpits,* quoted in Leonard Zeskind, *The "Christian Identity" Movement* (Atlanta: Division of Church and Society of the National Council of Churches of Christ in the U.S.A., 1986), p. 29.

2. *The Ku Klux Klan: A History of Racism and Violence* (Montgomery, Ala.: Klanwatch, 1988), p. 48.

3. Zeskind, *The "Christian Identity" Movement,* p. 29.

4. James Combs, "Jesus Was No Jew!" *Christian Vanguard,* August 1972, pp. 1 and 8.

5. For more on this document, see Herman Bernstein, *The Truth About "The Protocols of the Elders of Zion"* (New York: Ktav, 1972).

6. Zeskind, *The "Christian Identity" Movement,* p. 7.

7. *Hate Violence and White Supremacy: A Decade Review, 1980–1990,* Klanwatch Intelligence Report #47 (Montgomery, Ala.: Southern Poverty Law Center, 1989), p. 13.

8. Kevin Flynn and Gary Gerhardt, *The Silent Brotherhood* (New York: Signet, 1989), p. 69.

9. Leonard Zeskind, *Background Report on Racist and Anti-Semitic Organizational Intervention in the Farm Protest Movement* (Atlanta: Center for Democratic Renwal, 1985), p. 3.

10. From a Posse message broadcast over KTTL-FM, Dodge City, Kansas, and quoted by Frank L. Dorsey in "Who Is the Villain? The Posse Knows!" *engage/social action forum-131,* June 1987, p. 25.

11. Flynn and Gerhardt, *The Silent Brotherhood,* pp. 112–14.

12. *Hate Groups in America, A Record of Bigotry and Violence* (New York: Anti-Defamation League of B'nai B'rith, 1988), p. 52.

13. Ibid., p. 45.

14. Zeskind, *Background Report,* p. 1.

15. *Hate Groups in America, A Record of Bigotry and Violence,* p. 46.

16. Zeskind, *The "Christian Identity" Movement,* p. 43.

17. Zeskind, *Background Report,* p. 6.

18. Ibid., p. 7.

19. By *The Ku Klux Klan: A History of Racism and Violence* (Montgomery, Ala.: Klanwatch, 1988), p. 50.

20. From a letter by Butler, dated June 9, 1986, reprinted in "Aryan Nations Far-Right Underground Movement," an information package available from the Center for Democratic Renewal, Atlanta, pp. 7–9.

21. Butler made the claim in an appearance on the "Geraldo" television program, on November 20, 1990.

22. Flynn and Gerhardt, *The Silent Brotherhood,* p. 115.

23. Ibid., p. 309.

24. Ibid., p. 472.

25. *Hate and Violence and White Supremacy,* pp. 13–14.

8. NEW RECRUITS

1. See the Anti-Defamation League of B'nai B'rith, "The Hate Movement Today: A Chronicle of Violence and Disarray," an ADL Special Report, New York, 1988.

2. For more on Tom Metzger and "Race and Reason," see Elinor Langer, "The American Neo-nazi Movement Today," *The Nation*, July 16/23, 1990, pp. 82–107.

3. "Harvesting Young People's Hate," *Scholastic Update,* April 7, 1989, p. 6.

4. Leonard Zeskind, "Peddling Racist Violence for a New Generation" (Atlanta: Center for Democratic Renewal, 1987), p. 2.

5. Appearing on the "Donahue" television program, Multimedia Entertainment, January 19, 1987.

6. "Aryan Youth Movement White Student Union, Revolutionary Recruitment Issue," reprinted in "Neo-Nazi Skinheads & Youth Information Packet," available from the Center for Democratic Renewal, Atlanta, p. 39.

7. Ibid., p. 41. Withrow's speech was given at the 1986 Aryan Nations Congress.

8. "Donahue," January 19, 1987.

9. "Aryan Youth Movement White Student Union, Revolutionary Recruitment Issue," p. 39.

10. Anti-Defamation League of B'nai B'rith, "Skinheads Target the Schools," an ADL Special Report, New York (pages unnumbered).

11. "A Chilling Wave of Racism," *Time,* January 25, 1988, p. 57.

12. *Klanwatch Report: The Ku Klux Klan, A History of Racism and Violence,* 3rd ed. (Montgomery, Ala.: Southern Poverty Law Center, 1988), p. 54.

13. "Anti-Racist Skinheads Ready to Strike Back at Neo-Nazis," *Utne Reader,* May/June 1989, reprinted in "Neo-Nazi Skinheads & Youth Information Packet," p. 57.

14. "Harvesting Young People's Hate," p. 4.

15. "Anti-Racist Skinheads Ready to Strike Back at Neo-Nazis," p. 57.

16. *Hate Violence and White Supremacy: A Decade Review, 1980–1990,* Klanwatch Intelligence Report #47 (Montgomery, Ala.: Southern Poverty Law Center, 1989), pp. 27–28.

17. "Harvesting Young People's Hate," p. 6.

18. *Hate Violence and White Supremacy: A Decade Review, 1980–1990,* p. 17.

19. *Hate Groups in America, A Record of Bigotry and Violence* (New York: Anti-Defamation League of B'nai B'rith, 1988), pp. 59–60.

20. Kevin Flynn and Gary Gerhardt, *The Silent Brotherhood* (New York: Signet, 1989), p. 318.

21. *Hate Groups in America, A Record of Bigotry and Violence,* p. 57.

22. Ibid., p. 57.

9. WHY PEOPLE JOIN HATE GROUPS

1. Jeff Coplon, "Skinhead Nation," *Rolling Stone,* December 1, 1988.

2. Kirk Johnson, "A New Generation of Racism Is Seen," *New York Times,* August 27, 1989.

3. Coplon, "Skinhead Nation."

4. "Donahue," September 29, 1987.

5. "Today," May 21, 1991.

6. "Donahue," May 22, 1991.

7. Ibid.

8. Dees was speaking to the jury in the civil suit arising out of the murder of Mulugeta Seraw in Portland, which is dealt with in Chapter 11.

9. Interviewed on the "Geraldo" television program, November 20, 1990.

10. "Donahue," May 22, 1991.

11. *The Ku Klux Klan: A History of Racism and Violence* (Montgomery, Ala.: Klanwatch, 1988), p. 27.

12. Doug Clark, "Former Racist Returns to Say 'I'm Sorry,' " *Spokesman Review,* September 21, 1986.

10. WOLVES IN SHEEP'S CLOTHING

1. Kevin Flynn and Gary Gerhardt, *The Silent Brotherhood* (New York: Signet, 1989), pp. 37–38, and 42.

2. Ibid., p. 37.

3. For a more detailed criticism of La Rouche and the La Rouchies, see Dennis King, "Nazis Without Swastikas: The Lyndon La Rouche Cult and Its War on American Labor," published by the League for Industrial Democracy, n.d.

4. Ibid., p. 20.

5. *It's Not Populism* (Atlanta: Center for Democratic Renewal and Klanwatch, 1984), p. 5.

6. Richard N. Current, T. Harry Williams, and Frank Freidel, *American History: A Survey,* 4th ed. (New York: Knopf, 1975), p. 525.

7. *Ballot Box Bigotry: David Duke and the Populist Party* (Atlanta: Center for Democratic Renewal, 1989), p. 10.

8. George Will, "The Bad Seed of Our Politics," *Newsweek,* October 8, 1990, p. 80.

9. *Hate Groups in America, A Record of Bigotry and Violence* (New York: Anti-Defamation League of B'nai B'rith, 1988), p. 8.

10. "Donahue," May 19, 1989.

11. "After Duke, What Next?" *The Monitor,* November 1990, p. 2.

12. "Donahue," May 19, 1989.

13. Will, "The Bad Seed of Our Politics," p. 80.

14. See ibid., also Bill Turque (with Clara Bingham), "Duke Shows His True Colors," *Newsweek,* December 25, 1989, p. 53.

15. Ibid.

16. "Donahue," May 19, 1989.

17. Bill Nicols, "Duke Scores Big in Louisiana Loss," *USA Today*, October 8, 1990.

11. FIGHTING HATE

1. Anti-Defamation League of B'nai B'rith, "The Hate Movement Today: A Chronicle of Violence and Disarray," an ADL Special Report, New York, 1988, p. 3.

2. *Hate Violence and White Supremacy: A Decade Review, 1980–1990,* Klanwatch Intelligence Report #47 (Montgomery, Ala.: Southern Poverty Law Center, 1989), pp. 25–27.

3. "The Hate Movement Today," p. 1.

4. "Acquittal of the Haters," *Time*, April 18, 1988, p. 33.

5. *Hate Violence and White Supremacy*, pp. 19–20.

6. Ibid., p. 20.

7. *The Ku Klux Klan: A History of Racism and Violence* (Montgomery, Ala.: Klanwatch, 1988), p. 31.

8. "Donahue," May 22, 1991.

9. *Hate Violence and White Supremacy*, p. 22.

Bibliography

BOOKS

Allport, Gordon W. *The Nature of Prejudice*. Reading, Mass.: Addison-Wesley, 1954.

Coates, James. *Armed and Dangerous: The Rise of the Survivalist Right*. New York: Hill and Wang, 1987.

Cook, Fred J. *The Ku Klux Klan: America's Recurring Nightmare*. New York: Julian Messner, 1989.

Corcoran, James. *Bitter Harvest: Gordon Kahl and the Rise of the Posse Comitatus in the Heartland*. New York: Viking, 1990.

Dees, Morris, with Steve Fieffer. *A Season For Justice*. 1991.

Flynn, Kevin, and Gary Gerhardt. *The Silent Brotherhood: Inside America's Racist Underground*. New York: Signet, 1989.

Fry, Gladys-Marie. *Nightriders in Black Folk History*. Nashville: University of Tennessee Press, 1977.

Gossett, Thomas F. *Race: The History of an Idea in America*. Dallas: Southern Methodist University Press, 1963.

Holmes, Fred R. *Prejudice and Discrimination*. Englewood Cliffs, N.J.: Prentice Hall, 1970.

Jones, J. Harvey, Jr. *The Minuteman*. Garden City, N.Y.: Doubleday, 1968.

Jordan, Winthrop D. *The White Man's Burden: Historical Origins of Racism in the United States*. New York: Oxford University Press, 1974.

Lang, Susan S. *Extremist Groups in America*. New York: Watts, 1990.

Martinez, Thomas, with John Guinther. *Brotherhood of Murder*. New York: Pocket Books, 1988.

Wade, Wyn Craig. *The Fiery Cross*. New York: Simon and Schuster, 1987. (This book about the history of the KKK should not be confused with the Klan periodical of the same name.)

ARTICLES, REPORTS, AND SPECIAL PUBLICATIONS

"Aryan Nations Far-Right Underground Movement." Center for Democratic Renewal, Atlanta, 1986. (An information package containing several articles about the Aryan Nations, the Order, etc., along with a chronology of their activities, and related materials.)

"Background Report on Racist and Anti-Semitic Organizational Intervention in the Farm Protest Movement." Prepared by Leonard Zeskind. Center for Democratic Renewal, Atlanta, 1985.

"Background Report on Racist and Far-Right Organizing in the Pacific Northwest." Center for Democratic Renewal, Atlanta, 1988.

"Ballot Box Bigotry: David Duke and the Populist Party." Center for Democratic Renewal, Atlanta, 1989.

Coplon, Jeff. "Skinhead Nation," *Rolling Stone*, December 1, 1988.

"Harvesting Young People's Hate," *Scholastic Update*, special report, April 7, 1989.

Hate Groups in America, A History of Bigotry and Violence. New York: Anti-Defamation League of B'nai B'rith, 1988.

Hate Violence and White Supremacy: A Decade Review, 1980–1990. Klanwatch Intelligence Report #47. Montogomery, Ala.: Southern Poverty Law Center, 1989.

"It's Not Populism: America's New Populist Party: A Fraud by Racists and Anti-Semites." Center for Democratic Renewal and Klanwatch, Atlanta, 1984.

King, Dennis. "Nazis Without Swastikas," the League for Industrial Democracy. n.d.

The Ku Klux Klan: A History of Racism and Violence. Montgomery, Ala.: Klanwatch, a project of the Southern Poverty Law Center, 1988.

Langer, Elinor. "The American Neo-nazi Movement Today." *The Nation*, July 16/23, 1990.

"Mark of the Beast," a special edition of *Southern Exposure*, Summer 1980.

McLennan, Paul, and Trisha McLennan, with David Chalmers. *Solidarity or Division: The True Story of the Ku Klux Klan vs. Organized Labor.* Center for Democratic Renewal, Atlanta (sponsored by United Steelworkers of America), 1985.

"They Don't All Wear Sheets: A Chronology of Racist and Far Right Violence 1980–1986." Compiled by Chris Lutz, Center for Democratic Renewal. Published by the Division of Church and Society of the National Council of Churches of Christ in the U.S.A., Atlanta, 1987.

Zeskind, Leonard. *The "Christian Identity" Movement.* The Division of Church and Society of the National Council of Churches of Christ in the U.S.A., available from the Center for Democratic Renewal, Atlanta, 1986.

Zeskind, Leonard. "Peddling Racist Violence for a New Generation." Center for Democratic Renewal, Atlanta, 1987.

EXAMPLES OF HATE GROUP LITERATURE

Beam, Louis R., Jr. *Understanding the Struggle, or Why We Have to Kill the Bastards.* Hayden Lake: Aryan Nations, n.d.

Lane, David. *Life Law.* Hayden Lake: Church of Jesus Christ Christian-Aryan Nations, 1987.

MacDonald, Andrew. *The Turner Diaries.* Arlington, Va.: National Alliance, 1978.

The Spotlight, a periodical published by the Liberty Lobby, Washington, D.C.

The Thunderbolt, a periodical published by Thunderbolt, Inc., Marietta, Georgia. Described by an Anti-Defamation League publication as "the favorite hate sheet of the Ku Klux Klan, neo-Nazi bands and other bastions of extremism."

Index

Page numbers in italics refer to photographs.